A Dozen Dramatic Walks

in

Dorset

Simone Stanbrook–Byrne

and

James Clancy

CULM VALLEY PUBLISHING

Published by

Culm Valley Publishing Ltd
Culmcott House
Mill Street, Uffculme
Cullompton, Devon
EX15 3AT, UK
Tel: +44(0)1884 849085 Fax: +44(0)1884 840251
E-mail: info@culmvalleypublishing.co.uk
Website: www.culmvalleypublishing.co.uk

First published 2012

ISBN 978-1-907942-04-4 paperback

British Library Cataloguing-in-Publication Data
A catalogue record for this book is available from the British Library

Typeset by Culm Valley Publishing Ltd
Printed and bound by T.J. International Ltd, Padstow, Cornwall

Front cover image: The view east from the summit of Golden Cap (Walk 10)
Back cover image: Skirting the ramparts of Hod Hill (Walk 1)
All images used in this book are available as cards and prints from Culm Valley Publishing

Contents

Introduction

Writing this walking guide has been an enjoyable undertaking: the effort to attain the highest points, route-finding on elusive paths, fabulous views, country inns with open fires or sunny gardens – and the reward of ending the day where we intended.

By virtue of their nature 'dramatic walks' may involve tough terrain so whenever you embark on a walk, common sense must prevail: be properly shod and take care where you put your feet, be prepared for any kind of weather, take food and first aid supplies with you and make sure someone knows where you're going. Mobile phones are often useless in the middle of nowhere. Having said that, the drama is, for the most part, in the scenery rather than in the terrain.

We feel it's important that you take the **correct OS map** with you plus a **compass**, and are conversant with their use. Our sketch maps are precisely that – sketches – and are for rough guidance only and not necessarily to scale.

You know you've had a good day's walking when you get home safely at the end of it and haven't been overtaken by the drama.

Useful websites:
A useful site which gives tips for moorland treks is: www.tourbytor.co.uk/equip_walk.php. Although this is a Dartmoor site its information and advice is excellent for all walkers.

Follow the countryside code:
www.naturalengland.org.uk/ourwork/enjoying/countrysidecode/def ault.aspx

Our grateful thanks to:
Dr Phil Judkins, Chairman, Purbeck Radar Museum Trust;
Jill Exton, Rights of Way Officer (Operations) West Dorset;
Nic, Ella and William Clancy;
Tony Byrne.

Disclaimer

Points that should be borne in mind on any route – dramatic or not:

Public footpaths can be legally re-routed from the path shown on the map. In such cases they are usually clearly signposted. Where this has happened before the time of writing it has been noted in the text.

Most public footpaths are on private land. Please respect this.

Don't be surprised to find livestock grazing on public footpaths – and treat all animals with caution and respect.

If a field is planted with crops across a footpath, provision is usually made around the edge of the field.

Landmarks can change: trees and hedges may disappear; streams can dry up in warm weather or flood after heavy rain; stiles turn into gates and vice versa; fences appear where previously there was no boundary. Even views are different as the seasons progress. In such cases a modicum of common sense must be exercised – in conjunction with the map.

Public footpaths are at times blocked by barbed wire etc. Should this render the route impassable find the shortest detour around that section.

Please leave gates as you find them and if you have to climb them do so at the hinge end where it's stronger.

Exercise caution on wet stiles – they can be extremely slippery.

Take all your rubbish with you, please don't damage anything during the walk and don't pick plants.

Keep your dogs under proper control.

We hope that you enjoy these walks without mishap, but urge you to exercise common sense at all times. Neither the authors nor Culm Valley Publishing Ltd accepts responsibility for any misadventure that may occur during, or arise from, these walks and suggested routes.

Walk Locations

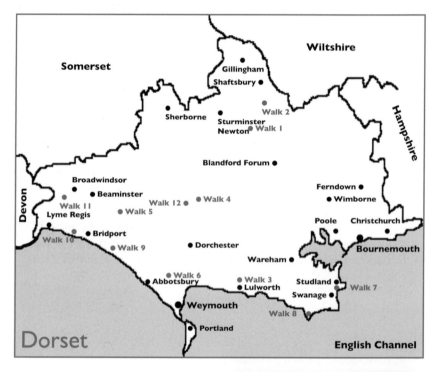

Walk 1 Child Okeford & Hambledon Hill
Walk 2 Compton Abbas & Melbury Beacon
Walk 3 Lulworth Cove & Durdle Door
Walk 4 Plush
Walk 5 Powerstock & Eggardon Hill
Walk 6 Portesham & the Hardy Monument
Walk 7 Studland, Old Harry & the Agglestone
Walk 8 Worth Matravers, St. Aldhelm's &
        Dancing Ledge
Walk 9 Burton Bradstock & Shipton Gorge
Walk 10 Charmouth, Seatown & Golden Cap
Walk 11 Pilsdon Pen
Walk 12 Cerne Abbas & Buckland Newton

Meeting of Ways (Walk 1)

Child Okeford & Hambledon Hill

Distance: 6¼ miles / 10km

This 'walk through time' is one of the more magnificent inland routes we know. Mighty hill forts and vast views combine to make for a spectacular walk. Some of the paths can be sticky underfoot and although there are ascents and descents they are a minor hurdle for the reward of reaching the heights.

Map: OS Explorer 118 Shaftesbury and Cranborne Chase 1:25 000

Start point: In Child Okeford near the war memorial. Post code: DT11 8ED. Grid ref: ST835128

Directions to start: Child Okeford is located in North Dorset approximately 6 miles north west of Blandford Forum. It can be reached off the A350/A357

Parking: On road in the village – please respect people's access to their driveways etc

Public Transport: Bus operators that pass through Child Okeford are: South West Coaches, Tourist Coaches and Damory Coaches. Timetables available online at www.travelinesw.com. Nearest railway station is Gillingham (8.5 miles)

Distance: 6¼ miles

Refreshments: Baker Arms, Child Okeford: 01258 860260; The Cake Tin Café, Gold Hill Organic Farm, Ridgeway Lane, Child Okeford: 01258 861119; The Cricketers, Iwerne Courtney: 01258 860421; The Saxon Inn, Gold Hill, Child Okeford, 01258 860310. There are plenty of superb picnic spots en route

Toilets: None en route

Nearby places to stay: The Saxon Inn, Gold Hill, Child Okeford, 01258 860310; Manor Barn B&B, Child Okeford, 01258 860638

Nearby places of interest: The North Dorset Railway Trust, Shillingstone Station, St. Patrick's Industrial Estate, Shillingstone, 01258 860696; Royal Signals Museum, Blandford Camp, Blandford Forum, 01258 482248

Possible birds include: Blackbird, black headed gull, blue tit, buzzard, carrion crow, great spotted woodpecker, great tit, green woodpecker, grey heron, jackdaw, long tailed tit, mute swan, nuthatch, pheasant, raven, redwing, robin, skylark, song thrush, woodpigeon, yellowhammer

Authors' tip: The Organic Farm at the junction of Gold Hill and Ridgeway Lane in Child Okeford is well worth a visit. In addition to the excellent organic produce on offer there is an art gallery, café and other small shops

Note: **Be aware: part of this route is across open moorland, so a map and compass are needed – and clear weather conditions**

From the war memorial walk away from the pub, out of the village and almost immediately take the right fork in the road towards the surgery, Iwerne Minster and Shaftesbury. Shortly after the surgery on the left you will see a track on the

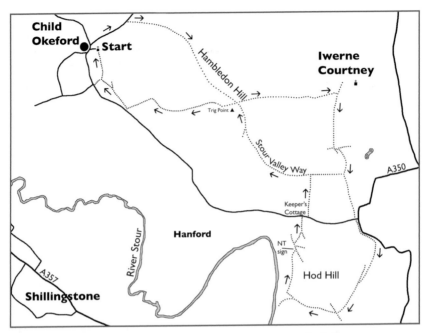

right leading to Manor Barn. A few metres along here on the left are some steps leading to a footpath. Go up here, through the kissing gate and follow the footpath ahead through the field with the lane down to your left. You are heading towards the massive, terraced heights of Hambledon Hill dominating the sky ahead of you. At the end of the field cross the stile by the gate in the left hand corner and a few metres beyond is another kissing gate leading to a footpath going right. Take this, walking away from the road.

This path leads to steps and a metal kissing gate with an information board beyond welcoming you to Hambledon Hill. You are now on access land and the path you want goes directly ahead up the hill, this is the Stour Valley Way. This climb isn't anything like as bad as it may look as there are earthy steps cut into the hillside which make for an easier ascent – we did it with heavy packs on and survived! Go up, heading for the highest point above the successive terraces of this ancient hill fort. Take a pause to look back at Child Okeford and its lovely Manor House just on the outskirts of the village.

Towards the top start to bear right (south east) still heading for the high part of the hill. Across to the right the view of the mighty ramparts extending round the fort is very dramatic and when you reach the top the all-surrounding, sweeping views are stunning. At the top turn right to walk along the hill fort, still heading towards higher ground though not steeply. To your left are views to the nearby villages of Iwerne Minster and Iwerne Courtney (also called Shroton). Wind your way above the craters and ramparts of the fort. Ahead in the distance you will see a trig point – this is what you're aiming for. Bear left to drop onto a bridleway which you will see heading for the trig point. This bridleway is just below the top of the hill with rising ground to its right. It leads to a gate beyond which is a fenced path to the trig. From here, on a clear day, you can see the Mendips to the north west, the Isle of Wight to the south east and Corfe Castle near the Dorset coast – although the two nice men whom we met said this might be reliant on a few beers. The dragon on the fingerpost denotes the Wessex Ridgeway Trail, a 137 mile footpath following ancient trade routes (see feature on Plush walk).

At the trig turn left towards Iwerne Courtney. This clear, easterly path drops down through a large field. At the bottom you meet a T-junction with a bridleway sporting an artistically carved fingerpost. If you wish to partake of vittles in Iwerne Courtney turn left into the village but otherwise the walk continues to the right, towards Steepleton Iwerne, following the path with a wall on the left which eventually gives way to metal palings.

The boundary on the left reaches a meeting of ways. Here, ignore the 90° left turn and take the second left track which goes obliquely left and uphill, as

On Hambledon Hill

Ramparts skirting Hod Hill

directed by a blue arrow. (There is another track going uphill but this is more ahead of you, and is to be ignored.) Follow the track with a tree-lined fence to your left beyond which you can see a pond with waterfowl. Within 60m you pass a double-pronged telegraph pole on your right with a blue bridleway arrow which will help to reassure you. You reach two bridleway gates in quick succession. After these continue in the same direction as before, along the bottom of the field with the hedge to your left. Ignore any footpaths off and at the end of the field emerge onto a lane.

Cross the lane bearing left a few metres to a gate onto another footpath. Walk through the field following its left boundary to the far side. The road is to your left and in the corner of the field go through a gate to join a path which quickly reaches another gate. Beyond this continue on the trodden path with the fence and road still to your left. This drops down to join a broad bridleway, still going in the same direction but which gradually bends away from the road and starts to climb. The rising ground to your right is the Roman fort of Hod Hill, there are good views to your left if the trees aren't in full leaf. The track leads to a gate, don't pass through but turn right as directed up to another gate where there is a National Trust sign denoting Hod Hill. Beyond this go straight ahead for 100m to climb up onto the ramparts of the fort (grid ref: ST858104).

Turn left along the top of the ramparts, heading in a westerly, clockwise direction on the trodden path. More superb views await you as you skirt the top of the hill fort, with its open grassy area to your right and big views to the left and ahead. Your walk around the ramparts is a distance of just over ½ mile (923m to be exact) and this is when your OS map is particularly useful. The path occasionally dips down to tracks and then rises again. Keep going round the ramparts, keeping a keen look out for a glimpse of the River Stour way below as it approaches the hill fort from the south. The rampart path bends round to head north and the river disappears from sight under the hill. You find you are walking with a steeply wooded hillside below to the left, you cannot see the river at this point. You may notice stone steps leading left off the ramparts, ignore these and keep going. When you see the river again, with the hamlet of Hanford beyond it, continue along the ramparts until you drop down to a chalky track leading left out of the hill fort, near grid ref: ST854109 at the north west corner of the fort. Keep your eyes peeled for the National Trust sign by a gate less than 100m away which you can see from the ramparts. Head for this.

Beyond the gate, follow the path initially beside woodland and a fence to the left. You drop down through a field into the valley and a broad path comes down to meet you from the right. Keep going down towards a gate in the treed boundary below you. Cross the lane beyond the gate towards Keepers Cottage. Beyond its entrance a bridleway goes into the field. Take this, following it uphill with a hedge to your left. This is a bit of a drag, up away from the road. It is still part of the Stour Valley Way with its kingfisher symbol.

Ignore a forestry track on the left and keep climbing until you find a corrugated iron barn. Beyond this turn left through a metal gate to then follow a path ahead with the fence on your right. It bends right and eventually reaches another metal gate beyond which is a slightly sunken track with the fence still to your right, the ground dropping away beyond it. Keep on the track until you meet another gate with a fingerpost. Go through here and ahead in the direction for Hambledon Hill. Soon you reach our old friend the trig point again.

From here go through the gate on the left and bear right across the field beyond in the direction shown by a blue bridleway arrow. You are once more heading towards the ramparts of Hambledon Hill. This line leads, in about 150m, to a gap in the fence with a path beyond heading out of the field. The path drops down, ramparts up to your right and lovely views to the left towards Child Okeford. At a metal gate pass through and continue on the narrower, fenced path. You reach another gate on the right with an info board about the area. Bear left here

Hambledon Hill

Regarded as one of the best hill forts in the country, this area has been a source of great archaeological discoveries. Carbon dating suggests initial occupation of the site during the late Neolithic era, around the 4th millennium BC when the area was still wooded. During the Bronze Age trees were cleared. There is evidence that  vines were cultivated here and the discovery of a male skeleton with arrow damage might indicate at least one period of skirmish. Greater evidence of occupation exists from the Iron Age when the fort's size was increased with the addition of more banks and ditches for defence against would-be attackers and possibly also as a display of power. It is thought that it was abandoned around 300BC, with the occupants possibly relocating to Hod Hill.

away from the hill, dropping beneath some lovely beech trees along a clear track. You reach a driveway beside two houses on the left. At the lane turn right and go immediately right again over a stepped stone stile to another footpath. This leads beside the lane with fields to the right and a rather grand old oak. The Manor House is over to the right with the church across the field.

The path ends at the garden of an attractive house. Two options face you. If you have a non-agile dog whom you can't lift (see * below)you will need to go left here to meet the lane, then right along the lane to follow it as it bends right back into the village and your car. Otherwise, go right to cross a stile into a small field. Bear diagonally right across the field to the corner of a hedge and fence then go left round this boundary to follow it towards the wall of the churchyard. In this wall you will find stone steps going up into the churchyard. *At about 4 feet high on the field side this wall is the canine challenge. Pandora, a fair-sized collie-dalmatian cross, spurred on by the prospect of getting left behind, cleared it in one bound – much to our astonishment. Walk through St. Nicholas' Churchyard to emerge at its main gate and you'll find yourself back near the war memorial.

Compton Abbas & Melbury Beacon
Distance: 4¼ miles / 6.8km

This is a walk of vast, panoramic views and wide open spaces. There are some ups and downs but they are a small price to pay for the scenery. The proximity of the tiny airfield means that you may have the fun of seeing small planes overhead.

Map: OS Explorer 118 Shaftesbury and Cranborne Chase 1:25 000

Start point: Car park and layby on the road ¼ mile from Compton Abbas Airfield. Post code: (of airfield) SP5 5AP. Grid ref: ST886187

Directions to start: See start point above

Parking: Car park and layby shown on OS map ¼ mile from Gore Clump and Compton Abbas Airfield on Spread Eagle Hill

Public Transport: Bus services that operate in the area are: South West Coaches and Damory Coaches. Timetables available online at www.travelinesw.com. Nearest railway station is Gillingham (6 miles)

Distance: 4¼ miles

Refreshments: Compton Abbas Airfield Café: 01747 811767 near the start and finish but nothing en route

Toilets: None en route

Nearby places to stay: The Chalet B&B, Christys Lane, Shaftesbury, 01747 853945; The Old Forge, Chapel Hill, Compton Abbas, 01747 811881

Nearby places of interest: Gold Hill Museum, 1 Gold Hill, Shaftesbury, 01747 852157; Shaftesbury Abbey, Park Walk, Shaftesbury, 01747 852910

Possible birds include: Blackbird, bullfinch, buzzard, carrion crow, chaffinch, goldfinch, great spotted woodpecker, great tit, house sparrow, jackdaw, kestrel, magpie, robin, siskin, skylark, song thrush

Authors' tip: Before or after your walk the renowned airfield restaurant is a must. Sit by the grassy runway and enjoy the buzz. You may even be tempted to a lesson in a Gypsy Moth

From the car park turn right along the path beside the road, which has been set aside by the National Trust to keep you out of the traffic. You are heading in a roughly southerly direction with good views to your right. Soon you reach a clump of trees opposite a turning left off the road which leads to the airfield. This area is Gore Clump. Turn right here, away from the road, and follow the path alongside the fence on your right. Before you get far from the road you will see an information board beyond the trees telling you about Fontmell and Melbury Downs which were purchased in memory of the author Thomas Hardy to protect his much-loved landscapes.

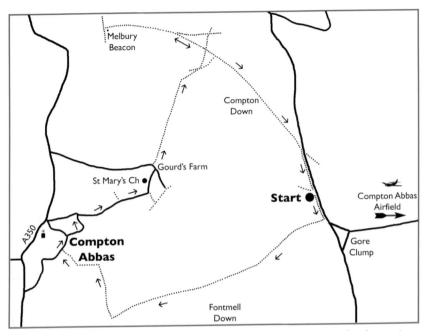

Follow the fence on your right along this broad, grassy path as it leads you into stunning views with the striking drop into Longcombe Bottom on your left. You are heading towards trees in the middle distance and the village of Compton Abbas comes into view down on the right. Look out for a chubby little boundary stone to the right of the path, 500m after leaving the road. Just beyond him bear slightly right on the path to reach a gate on the right. Pass through here then go left in the same direction as before, now with the fence on the left, to skirt the trees, keeping them to your left. Look out for more old boundary stones along this line.

The trees on your left come to an end, keep ahead on the clear path ignoring any gates or paths to the left. The path you are on starts to drop, bearing slightly right with an occasional blue bridleway arrow. You are heading down to Compton Abbas. About 350m from the end of the trees you reach a gate with a National Trust sign indicating that you are leaving Fontmell Down. The path beyond the gate leads into a field. Keep ahead across the field with the fence to your left. At the end of the field turn right, staying in the same field and keeping its boundary to your left. Head down to a gate with Melbury Hill towering above the village ahead of you. Pass through the gate and walk through the next field, fence still to your left with lovely, undulating views beyond. You reach a small gate on your left leading onto a blue-arrowed bridleway out of the field but still going in the same direction. Take this attractive path and follow its bends until you reach a lane. Turn right, this is Compton Abbas.

Walk through the village, ignoring a turning left in 100m, until you reach a T-junction by a post box. Turn right along the lane, passing the houses of Twintown in about 200m and continuing until you reach the remains of St. Mary's Church on the left. Notice the old mounting block by its gate.

From the church continue along the lane to a grassy triangle about 40m further on. At this T-junction turn left and within 30m go right along a track. In another 20m keep ahead through a gate and follow the track ahead which leads towards the saddle-like dip between two high hills ahead of you. This is a good, clear route through a broad 'bowl' within hills. At the end of the field the track leads to a gate, beyond which is another gate to the right leading onto a bridleway. A National Trust board denotes that this is Melbury Hill.

Follow the track uphill in the direction of the bridleway arrow. When you need to pause for breath enjoy the views behind. You meet a broad crossing track, turn right along it and continue uphill. You reach a fence ahead. Turn left and start to ascend to the heady heights of Melbury Hill, passing a bridleway gate on the right and keeping the fence to your right. If you don't wish to undertake this

Across Fontmell Down

St Mary's Church

The Grade I listed, 15thC tower is all that remains of the original mediæval St. Mary's Church in East Compton. Once a much-loved church which had replaced an earlier wooden church, by the middle of the 19thC the thatched building had fallen into disrepair and it was decided to replace it with a modern church. Some of the fittings from this old church, including the 1000 year old font, were transferred to the new St. Mary's Church at the other end of the village when that was built between 1866  and 1868 using some stone from this old building. Graves, old memorials and a mediæval preaching cross still adorn the old churchyard. One of the gravestones, to Robert Parham who died in July 1867, is quite close to the tower and would have been within the area of the nave indicating that the churchyard was still in use at this time but the church was no longer standing. Apparently a pear tree once grew out of the tower roof, blossoming annually. It was removed after snow-damage in 1945. These fascinating ruins are now in the care of the Society for the Protection of Ancient Buildings.

climb wait for us at the bridleway gate. If you are going up you will be well-rewarded at the top.

When you reach the trig-point at 263m drink in the expansive, 360° panorama. It's awesome in the accurate sense of the word. The town to the north is Shaftesbury beyond which is Wiltshire and much closer to hand, also north of the ridge as you ascend, is the village of Melbury Abbas.

From the trig point cross the stile and enjoy the airy descent back to the bridleway gate. Here you pick up the faint-hearted who didn't want the climb and missed the fun, and continue ahead with the fence on your right. The path ascends again and when you crest the brow of the hill you will see the airfield ahead in the distance, with the road before it and the parking area. Follow the path beside the fence until you reach the road, at which point turn right along the designated path to arrive safely back at the car park.

View from Melbury Beacon

The Moon!

Walk 3

Lulworth Cove & Durdle Door
Distance: 4½ miles / 7¼km

The Jurassic Coast is spectacular and this walk encompasses one of the more striking features of it: Durdle Door. The route brings you to this point from inland so the first view is breathtaking. The area is beautiful not just for its coastal scenery – at the right time of year wildflowers abound and it can be a birdwatchers' and entomologists' paradise. You may also see adders and roe deer. The field paths can be slightly overgrown but generally they are good and easy to follow although there are three uphill stretches. You may hear gunfire from the military training ranges of nearby Lulworth Camp, but the walk doesn't intrude on them!

Map: OS Explorer OL15 Purbeck & South Dorset 1:25 000

Start point: In West Lulworth outside the church. Post code: BH20 5RY. Grid ref: SY823807

Directions to start: West Lulworth is in the Purbeck district about 12 miles south east of Dorchester. It can be accessed from the A352

Parking: On road parking at Church Road outside the church

Public Transport: Bus operators that pass through West Lulworth are: First in Dorset & South Somerset, Dorset Community Transport and Damory Coaches. Timetables available online at www.travelinesw.com. Nearest railway stations are Wool (4 miles), Moreton (5.9 miles) and Wareham (7.4 miles)

Distance: 4½ miles

Refreshments: The Castle Inn, West Lulworth, 01929 400311; Lulworth Cove Inn, Lulworth Cove, 01929 400333

Toilets: At Lulworth Cove

Nearby places to stay: Bindon Bottom B&B, Main Road, West Lulworth, 01929 400 256; The Old Barn, Main Road, West Lulworth, 01929 400305

Nearby places of interest: Lulworth Castle and Park, Lulworth Castle, East Lulworth, 01929 400352; Monkey World Ape Rescue Centre, Wareham, 01929 462537; The Tank Museum, Bovington, 01929 405096

Possible birds include: Blackbird, buzzard, carrion crow, chaffinch, chiffchaff, dunnock, goldfinch, greenfinch, gulls of various hue, house martin, house sparrow, jackdaw, kestrel, magpie, robin, shag, skylark, song thrush, sparrowhawk, starling, swallow, swift, woodpigeon, wren

Authors' tip: When the army aren't firing consider an excursion to the famous Fossil Forest to the east of Lulworth Cove. Here, on a wide ledge above the sea, are the fossilized remains of trees dating from the Upper Jurassic period (135 million years old). Check for latest information on access times on 01929 404819

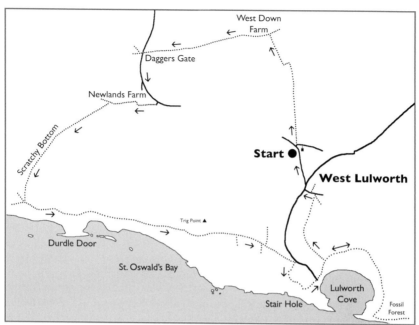

From the church in West Lulworth seek the footpath leading off the road at the junction of Church Road and West Road. This junction is just beyond the west end of the churchyard. A small, stone waymarker tells you this path goes to West Down Farm, ½ a mile away. A short stretch of track goes up to a farm gate. Beyond here follow the hedge on the right as it climbs steadily, passing through the remains of an old hedge boundary which wanders over from the left. Continue up to reach a stile. Pause and admire the views back across the village and towards Lulworth Cove beyond. To the right is the Isle of Portland.

Keep going up through the next field with the hedge still to the right. At the top go left, in the same field with the hedge still on your right and then within 50m go right again to a gap in the corner with footpath arrows. Beyond here continue through the next field in the same line as before, you will see the buildings of West Down Farm ahead to the left. The path exits the field onto a track, turn left along it, passing the farmhouse on your right. You now follow the track for almost 1km until you reach the lane.

This is Daggers Gate. Turn left along the lane, looking out for traffic, and in just over 200m you reach Newlands Farm. Stay on the lane past the farm, and beyond it you reach the entrance to Durdle Door Holiday Park. A public footpath sign directs you along their drive. Follow it, and as it swings left keep straight ahead through the gate into Newlands Farm, passing barns on the right and heading towards the farmhouse. At the farmhouse go right, away from it, then in about 15m left on the track, clearly signed as a footpath towards Ringstead.

As you continue along the track you leave the farm buildings behind. Caravans are down to the left but the panorama across the coast to Portland is lovely. Also glance behind for good views. Within 300m of the farm you find a footpath going left, another attractive round-topped waymarker is beside the path here and on the gate is a yellow 'moth' footpath arrow, denoting that this is part of the West Lulworth Country Trail. Pass through the small footpath gate (not the farm gate onto the track) and go diagonally down the field towards the trees to the right of the caravans.

This line leads you to a gate with a footpath arrow. Continue beyond it on the track with the fence to your right, you are now heading down a path into the delightfully named Scratchy Bottom (ointment is available), which is curiously devoid of prickly vegetation. Rising ground surrounds this area, forming an attractive 'bowl'. The steep hill immediately to your left is Newlands Warren.

Keep following the clear path with the fence on your right and Newlands Warren to your left, swinging left with the path and gently dropping down towards the coast. When you reach the coast pause by the fence (where a sign warns you of unstable cliffs) to enjoy the views. The mighty white cliff to your right, Swyre

Observing Scratchy Bottom

Swyre Head, Bat's Head and Bat's Hole

Head, is part of the Jurassic Coast (see feature on Studland walk) and this is the highest vertical chalk cliff in Dorset.

The walk goes left (east), the sea to your right. Remember to glance back from time to time as you walk – the coastline is spectacular. Soon you see the amazing sight of Durdle Door. Pause and ponder. Behind you along the coast, below the cliffs of Bat's Head, you can see a dinky Durdle Door known as Bat's Hole.

Continue on the coast path beyond Durdle Door towards Lulworth Cove, just over a mile away. Soon the stony path swings inland and the coast path proper forks right, staying closer to the sea and this is what you need to follow. Continue along the clear path, passing through a gate and climbing steadily. As the path starts to drop a magnificent view opens ahead, towards the distinctive Lulworth Cove and along the coastline. Descend towards the buildings, crossing the car park and looking for a three-way fingerpost directing you towards Stair Hole and Lulworth Cove. Follow its direction and look for the next multi-way fingerpost opposite the Lulworth Cove Inn, beside the Heritage Centre. Take the right hand option on the coast path, still heading for Stair Hole and Lulworth Cove and away from the Inn.

Behind the Heritage Centre another post directs you up and left (not directly left) towards the sea, still heading for Stair Hole which you now quickly reach.

Durdle Door & Lulworth Cove

Durdle Door (see colour plates) is a limestone arch, formed by varying rates of sea erosion from what was once a cave. Close examination reveals holes left by fossilised trees. Geologists are working to preserve the arch against the power of the elements which try to reduce it. The word 'durdle' derives from Old English 'thirl' which roughly translates as 'pierced' (cf Thurlestone Rock in Devon).

Lulworth, with its narrow opening and circular formation, is one of the world's finest examples of a cove. Coves are formed when softer rock is eroded faster than the surrounding, more durable rock and Lulworth's circular shape is caused by the arcing of the waves after they enter the cove.

Cliffs near Durdle Door

Stair Hole

Beyond it follow the coast path beside the prominent lump of stone, unveiled by the Prince of Wales in 2002, towards the cove. Drop down to the lane running into the cove and then ascend the steps on the other side of the lane. You have good views of the cove as you climb. The path enters under trees and continues uphill. You reach a kissing gate and here have options.

If you wish to follow the Authors' Tip go right, uphill beside the trees, to achieve more very fine views across the cove and to reach the Fossil Forest (if the army isn't firing!). However, you will need to return to this kissing gate. From the gate the walk goes ahead, away from the trees and up a short slope before winding gently downhill. Rising land is to your right and a fence and trees are to your left. At a multi-way fingerpost keep straight on for West Lulworth. This line leads to a footpath gate beyond which a path drops down towards houses. Another fingerpost is followed by a gate near some cottages – Sunnyside Terrace.

Go left along the track away from the cottages and at the right turning for the Youth Hostel keep straight ahead. You reach the lane at Cove House, cross over and turn right, then immediately left along Church Road and back to the start.

Plush

Distance: 4½ miles / 7¼km

This lovely, short route follows the rim of hills surrounding the delightful village of Plush which can be glimpsed frequently throughout the walk. Tiny and tucked away, Plush could easily be missed, which would be a great shame. The Brace of Pheasants is a lovely 16thC Inn and a bit of a Mecca for walkers. It was once two cottages and became an Inn around the time of WWII when the owner of the local estate wished to keep his workers on his own patch rather than letting them spend their money in neighbouring villages. The church, St. John the Baptist, was deconsecrated in the latter part of the 20thC. The lovely, mid 19thC building was then bought by the owners of the local Manor and has now been reborn as a prestigious concert venue. Although a reasonably easy-to-follow route, it's always an idea to have a map and compass to help confirm your position.

Map: OS Explorer 117 Cerne Abbas & Bere Regis 1:25 000

Start point: From outside The Brace of Pheasants public house. Post code: DT2 7RQ. Grid ref: ST714021. Also limited street parking – exercise courtesy

Directions to start: Plush is a hamlet in central Dorset situated 9½ miles north east of Dorchester. It can be accessed from the B3143 at Piddletrenthide

Parking: The landlord at The Brace of Pheasants is happy to allow parking for walkers provided refreshments are taken at the pub

Public Transport: Plush is served by South West Coaches and Damory Coaches. Timetables available online at www.travelinesw.com. Nearest railway stations: Dorchester West, Dorchester South and Maiden Newton (all 7.6 miles)

Distance: 4½ miles

Refreshments: The Brace of Pheasants, Plush, 01300 348357

Toilets: None en route

Nearby places to stay: The Brace of Pheasants, Plush, 01300 348357; Longpuddle B&B, Piddlehinton, 01300 348532

Nearby places of interest: Athelhampton House and Gardens, Athelhampton, 01305 848363; Tolpuddle Martyrs Museum, Tolpuddle, 01305 848237

Possible birds include: Blackbird, buzzard, carrion crow, chiffchaff, magpie, partridge (red-legged and grey), pheasant, skylark, swallow, woodpigeon, wren, yellowhammer

Authors' tip: Every summer the village hosts classical, contemporary and jazz concerts. Further information at http://www.musicatplush.net

Note: Be aware: part of this route is across open moorland, so a map and compass are useful – and clear weather conditions

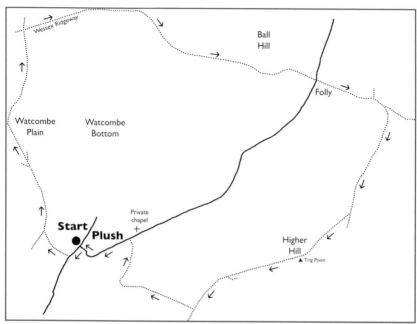

From The Brace of Pheasants walk along the lane signed for Piddletrenthide and Dorchester. In 100m, just as you leave the village, you will find a bridleway on the right signposted for Church Hill. Take this and follow it, ignoring the footpath going left after 200m and staying on the broad, rising bridleway through woodland. Pass through one gate and continue uphill to a second gate, 500m from the footpath junction.

Beyond this gate you enter a huge field which is the access land of Watcombe Plain. There are fabulous, sweeping views down to Watcombe Bottom on the right. Walk ahead from the gate to a stubby, stone marker about 30m away on which a blue arrow points you obliquely left to follow the broad, if rather indistinct, grassy track. (There is also a track going ahead to the right of the stone which you don't want). The track you are following rises across the plain and levels slightly in about 300m, swinging right as it is joined by another track from the left. You'll see a ruined barn way down on the right. The ground continues to rise gently through this enormous field of scrubby trees and gorse, and you're heading roughly north towards the far boundary of the field. In this boundary you will see two distinct gaps, you are aiming for the one on the right, almost 800m from the gate at which you entered this field.

Beyond the gap walk straight across the field to a stile with an adjacent fingerpost which has no fingers. Here you will find an information board about Harvey's

Farm and a map which gives a rather unclear indication of where you are and is best ignored, as are the arrows attached to the stile! Your grid ref here is ST711035. Don't cross the stile! Turn right, staying in the same field and keeping the hedge and fence to your left. This is now the Wessex Ridgeway, a lovely section of the walk along Church Hill. You are heading slightly north of east.

This long field narrows and curves right towards its end – you'll find yourself walking between woodland, Hill Wood to the left and Watcombe Wood to the right. At the end of the field you find a farm gate leading to a track. Follow this to then enter another field where an arrow directs you to follow the hedge on the left as it curves away (its direction is just south of due east). A slightly indistinct track beside the hedge takes you to the end of the field where another gate and arrow await. Beyond here follow the track, still on the Wessex Ridgeway and dropping downhill. You reach another gate onto a narrow path, continue under trees, still downhill. The path broadens out to become a track, passing a house on the right and arriving at a lane.

This is Folly. Cross the lane and continue on the bridleway beyond, passing the entrance to Folly Farmhouse. This track is signed for Dorset Gap and climbs steadily. Keep going, ignoring a footpath through a gate on the left after 350m. Another 50m beyond this the bridleway forks. There is a three-way fingerpost

The Brace of Pheasants

Plush nestles in a bowl of hills

here, which at the time of writing was thoroughly buried in the overgrown hedge. Go right here, quickly reaching a gate with an adjacent stile. Beyond the gate follow the well-trodden path which initially goes slightly left then right along the line of the field's left boundary – the boundary is above to your left and the path is climbing slightly. This narrow, sometimes sticky bridleway keeps rising through an area of scrub and trees. You may find it easier to walk on top of the raised bank to your right. If you're walking it in the summer and it's still muddy look out for spotted orchids to take your mind off the problem.

Eventually the path emerges into a more open area with sweeping views to your right. 400m from the gate at which this path started you will find the fence on the left going left at 90° to the path. At this point walk straight ahead across the field for just over 300m, with rising land to your left and a slope down to the right. The path rises gently to reach a treed boundary (this is the left hand field boundary which comes in again to meet the path). Here you will find a four-way fingerpost. Take the bridleway towards Doles Ash Farm, staying in the same field and following the line of the left boundary with lovely views away to your right.

The trees on your left come to an end and on the other side of the fence you will see a trig point. Keep on the path, going downhill beside the fence to reach a gate. Pass through and keep on in the same line, the fence still to your left. This reaches another gate with a clear path beyond it heading straight across the field to the right hand end of a copse. When you reach the trees walk beside them for less than 100m and at their corner, as the bridleway goes left, you will find a footpath heading right. Take this. (At the time of writing whoever farmed this field had made one of the best provision for rights of way of any Dorset farmer we encountered – thank you!)

So, go right on this footpath and at the end of the field cross the stile to keep straight down the next field in the same line. Plush is below you and you can see its now-converted church nestling in the trees down to the right. The 'bowl' in which Plush sits is very obvious from this point. You reach a stile, follow the direction of its yellow arrow as it points you left. The path then winds right to drop down to the corner of the field and thence to the lane. Here, if you wish to peer through the gates at the old church, go right for 70m, but the walk turns left along the lane, back to the centre of the village and the Inn.

Trade Routes

The Wessex Ridgeway, part of the more extensive Great Ridgeway, is a 137 mile footpath following old trade routes, a network of which would have been established from prehistoric times to serve the scattered but populous settlements of Neolithic and Bronze Age England. Use of these routes, started by early peoples, continued over successive centuries. High, open countryside provided easier and safer travelling than muddy,  wooded valleys. Livestock, crops, minerals and other goods would have been brought by these ways to supply our ancestors, linking pockets of population with each other and with the ports so that goods could also be imported/exported. Artefacts found during excavations indicate that overseas trade took place. Burial mounds or tumuli are often found along the line of these old routes, memorials to a civilisation now long-gone. The two-legged dragon on the symbol is a wyvern, a creature associated with the ancient Kingdom of Wessex.

Powerstock & Eggardon Hill

Distance: 6½ miles / 10½km

This superb walk starts in a very pretty village with an appealingly-chiming church clock if you can arrange to be there at the top of the hour. Part of the walk is along one of the most magnificently-situated (and very quiet) lanes we have ever encountered, running below the ramparts of a hill fort with stunning views across the surrounding countryside and no tree roots to trip over while you're marvelling at it. As ever, good views require a bit of ascent. There is the added advantage of three possible refreshment stops en route in attractive hamlets.

Map: OS Explorer 117 Cerne Abbas & Bere Regis 1:25 000

Start point: From the church in Powerstock. Post code: DT6 3TD. Grid ref: SY516961

Directions to start: Powerstock is a village in south west Dorset situated 4½ miles north east of Bridport. It can be accessed from the A3066

Parking: On street parking is usually possible in the centre of the village close to the church, with consideration for residents

Public Transport: The only bus-service passing through Powerstock is the number 73 operated by South West Coaches. Timetables available online at www.travelinesw.com. Nearest railway station is Maiden Newton (5.3 miles)

Distance: 6½ miles

Refreshments: The Marquis of Lorne, Nettlecombe, 01308 485236; The Spyway Inn, Askerswell, 01308 485250; The Three Horseshoes, Powerstock, 01308 485328

Toilets: None en route unless you're stopping for refreshment at the pubs

Nearby places to stay: The Marquis of Lorne, Nettlecombe, 01308 485236; The Spyway Inn, Askerswell, 01308 485250; The Three Horseshoes, Powerstock, 01308 485328

Nearby places of interest: Bridport Museum, The Coach House, Gundry Lane, Bridport, 01308 458703; Mapperton House and Gardens, Mapperton, nr Beaminster, 01308 862645

Possible birds include: Blackbird, buzzard, carrion crow, chaffinch, chiffchaff, goldfinch, gulls of various hue, house sparrow, jackdaw, kestrel, magpie, skylark, song thrush, swallow, woodpigeon, wren, yellowhammer

Authors' tip: We recommend a visit to Mapperton House and Gardens. Before setting out on this 6-mile excursion north of Powerstock first check opening times: http://www.mapperton.com/visitus.html

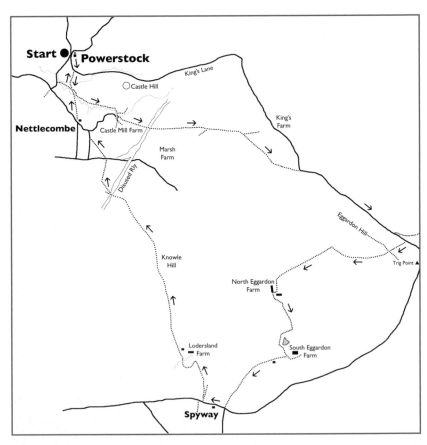

From the centre of Powerstock, below the church, take the road uphill signed towards Whetley and Eggardon Hill. The church wall is on your left and you almost immediately pass the Three Horseshoes on your right. The road starts to descend and about 50m from the Inn you will find a footpath on the right. Take this, towards Nettlecombe, the path leading down to a footbridge followed by a gate. Bear left after the gate to walk the length of this long, narrow field. You may hear the stream down to your right and wooded slopes rise to either side.

At the end of the field cross the stile to find a blue-arrowed bridleway beyond. Go right and follow the path with a stream down to the right, approaching attractive Castle Mill Farm, named for the site of the Norman motte and bailey castle to the north. Cross a footbridge towards the house and turn left at the end of the bridge. Just beyond the end of the house you find an ascending footpath going right off the track, take it. Climb up under trees to a stile, after which follow the left boundary through the field. At the end cross a stile and the narrow path beyond goes over an old bridge. Below this, if there's not too much overgrowth, you may glimpse the line of a disused railway which was in use until 1975. Beyond the bridge cross another stile and follow the field hedge on your left to yet another stile. Keep on in the same line, Eggardon Hill is ahead of you, and soon you cross the grassy track to Marsh Farm, away to the right.

Keep going beyond the farm track, with the field hedge still to your left, to reach another stile. Continue beyond it enjoying good views to your right and behind when you pause for breath. Yet another stile leads to a narrow path under trees and after these a further stile takes you to a broad track. Keep ahead on this, ignoring any footpaths off until you reach a gate. There's a nice view back to Powerstock Church from here, nestling in the valley. You reach the road, King's Lane, keep ahead along it climbing steadily, with the heights of Eggardon Hill to your right.

As you ascend the views to your left become enormous. Savour them as you follow this lane for almost ¾ mile – it's almost a shame when you turn off! But turn off you must, when you reach a prominent bridleway sign pointing right. Follow its direction through the field along the clear path heading south west

The view from King's Lane

Bridleway beside the ramparts of Eggardon Hill

and slightly uphill. You will see a trig point away to your left in this field and as you crest the hill the sea comes into view.

At the end of the field exit through a gate and turn right on the track. In about 50m you reach another gate and stile ahead leading onto a broad bridleway track descending to the left. There is an adjacent stile at 90° on the right which leads up onto a footpath crossing Eggardon Hill – you are at liberty to explore if you wish to go across the top of the hill fort, although this isn't part of the walk. Your route continues by bearing left beyond the gate, following the bridleway track as it descends beside the ramparts, keeping the fence and sweeping views to your left.

Keep on this path for just over 500m as it descends and eventually bends left to reach a gate on the left with a blue arrow – make sure you get the right gate with the arrow! Beyond here walk down the field with its boundary to your right – when we were here in June this field was full of poppies. Keep on in this line until you reach a concrete drive at North Eggardon Farm. Turn left, passing the barns on your right.

The drive leads you into a yard, turn right and then left in about 20m, working your way between the buildings then walking away from the farm, still along the track. In about 75m this starts to swing left towards the entrance to a house, at which point you keep ahead on the grassy track, passing the house and its garden

Durdle Door (Walk 3)

Cerne Giant from viewpoint (Walk 12)

Foxgloves near Studland (Walk 7)

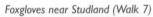

Descending Pilsdon Pen (Walk 11)

Eggardon Hill from South Eggardon Farm (Walk 5)

Ramparts at Hod Hill (Walk 1)

Watcombe Bottom (Walk 4)

Hambledon Hill (Walk 1)

Chilcombe Hill (Walk 9)

Pinnacles near Old Harry (Walk 7)

Lulworth Cove (Walk 3)

Field path towards Seatown (Walk 10)

Powerstock (Walk 5)

Stegosaurus enjoying the view (Walk 6)

Chapman's Pool (Walk 8)

on your left. At the end of the garden you enter a field. Bear right through the field on a level path which then drops towards trees in the boundary, just over 100m from entering the field. Here you will find a bridleway gate.

Follow the narrow path beyond through the trees. It leads into a field which can be quite marshy. Pick your way down the field following the line of the fence on your right. Just after an opening into the field on the right you will find a bridleway gate, also on the right. Go through this, following the path beyond for 75m, and as the fence on your left bends away you will see a blue arrow on a post, directing you left, to still follow the line of this fence. The path begins to ascend and you may get glimpses of an attractive pond beyond the fence. The path rises to meet another blue arrowed gate.

Beyond here continue up the next field, still with the boundary to your left. You meet the drive to South Eggardon Farm, turn right along it — this is still a bridleway. Pass South Eggardon Cottage on your left and keep going until you reach the lane. Turn right along it and you will pass the Spyway Inn on your left. Rest or continue, as the mood dictates. Dogs are allowed in the lovely garden.

About 100m beyond the inn you find a bridleway going right. Take this, towards Powerstock, and in 20m the path splits, with the blue-arrowed bridleway going

Below Eggardon Hill

Eggardon Hill

Hill forts were our ancestors' refuges, occupying high ground for ease of defence against would-be attackers. Some theories also suggest they were enlarged and enhanced as a display of power by tribal chiefs. Most enjoy superb, surrounding views and Eggardon is no exception. Dating back to the Iron Age it was in use  around 300BC and encloses Bronze Age burial mounds. It was also the location of the local 'moot' or council meeting place during Saxon times. This hill fort encompasses old field boundaries and an intriguing octagonal feature which once housed a stand of trees, used for sea navigation by local smugglers around the end of the 18thC. These features can be hard to discern under the growth of vegetation.

right and a yellow-arrowed footpath going left. Go left on the footpath following a clear track through the field as you approach Lodersland Farm, passing under wires as you go. When the track swings left after 250m, stay with it, ignoring the ahead option and turning back on yourself, approaching the wires again. Keep on the track as it bends right and starts to climb towards a breeze block and corrugated iron barn. About 70m from this right bend (you're walking away from the wires) you will see a left fork. Take this, passing the barn over to your right.

You enter a field with a rather broken down yellow arrow on the gate. Follow its direction bearing slightly right across the field – ahead of you to the right is the woodland of Knowle Hill. At the top of the field pass through the gate and now follow the line of the right hand boundary of the field beyond, still approaching the woodland. Keep going up, enjoying the surrounding views and at the top pass through to the next field, the track follows the right hand boundary with the woodland now to your right. From here you keep on the track through three more fields until it drops to a broad crossing track – the old railway line which you passed over earlier. This is one mile from the barn at Lodersland Farm.

Cross the old railway and keep ahead for less than 10m where you find a small path on the right, leaving the track. Take this, a lovely path under trees, for about 100m. It leads into an open field, walk across this, bearing very fractionally right, to a stile on the far side. Glance up right here – Eggardon Hill is watching over you.

Cross the stile and the lane beyond to enter another field in which you go immediately left over another stile. Here you enter a playing field encompassing football and cricket pitches. Walk diagonally right across the field to a stile in the middle of the fence. You are approaching the pretty hamlet of Nettlecombe and can see the tower of Powerstock Church ahead of you. After the stile keep going in the same line to the corner of the field where you find a stile and steps down to the lane.

At the lane turn right and in about 50m, in the middle of Nettlecombe, bend left with the lane to reach The Marquis of Lorne. Immediately beyond him turn right along the track off the lane then walk through the field with its boundary on your right. Powerstock is across the valley ahead of you. As the path starts to drop you will see a gate in the bottom boundary ahead, passing into woodland. Aim for this bottom gate (there is another footpath higher up on the right which you ignore).

Beyond the gate follow the narrow path beyond to cross a footbridge. After this you enter a field which you should recognise from earlier in the walk. Continue ahead across the field towards the trees in the opposite boundary, passing the corner of the fence on your right, where you will find a gate onto a footbridge. You crossed this in the other direction a while ago. From here retrace your steps across the bridge and up the path to the lane near the Three Horseshoes. Turn left along the lane, back to the church and your start point.

Walk 6
Portesham & the Hardy Monument
Distance: 7 miles / 11¼km

This glorious walk encompasses areas of Dorset used as locations in the 1967 film "Far from the Madding Crowd", starring Alan Bates, and adapted from Thomas Hardy's novel of the same name. The wildlife is good – you may see roe deer. Quite a bit of history is encountered on this route and there are some lovely stretches of dry stone walling, an historic part of the landscape. In places this has broken down and been quick-fixed with modern stock-proof fencing. Be prepared for some ascents – the resulting views are magnificent. Although not particularly difficult to navigate it is, as always, an idea to have the relevant map with you and a compass in case you need to verify your direction.

Map: OS Explorer OL15 Purbeck and South Dorset 1:25 000

Start point: Outside the King's Arms in Front Street, Portesham. Post code: DT3 4ET. Grid ref: SY602857

Directions to start: Portesham is a village situated near the south coast of Dorset. It is roughly 7 miles south west of Dorchester and can be accessed from the A35

Parking: On street near the King's Arms in Portesham

Public Transport: Bus operators that pass through Portesham are: First in Dorset & South Somerset and Damory Coaches. Timetables available online at www.travelinesw.com. Nearest railway stations are Upwey (4.6 miles), Dorchester West (6 miles), Weymouth (6.2 miles)

Distance: 7 miles

Refreshments: The Kings Arms, 2 Front Street, 01305 871342. There is often a refreshments van serving tea and coffee at the Hardy Monument

Toilets: None en route

Nearby places to stay: The Kings Arms, 2 Front Street, 01305 871342; Corton Farm, Friar Waddon, 01305 815784

Nearby places of interest: Abbotsbury Subtropical Gardens, Bullers Way, Abbotsbury, 01305 871387; Abbotsbury Swannery, New Barn Road, Abbotsbury, 01305 871858

Possible birds include: Blackbird, buzzard, carrion crow, collared dove, great tit, gulls of various hue, kestrel, long tailed tit, magpie, pheasant, red-legged partridge, skylark, swift, willow warbler, wren, yellowhammer

Authors' tip: After skirting Corton Hill ensure you stop at the delightful St. Bartholomew's Chapel for a peek inside

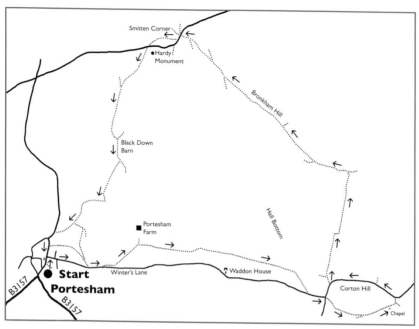

Walk away from the centre of this attractive village along the main road (Front Street) passing The Kings Arms on the right and St. Peter's Church on the left. A short distance beyond this turn right along Winters Lane. Ignore the first bridleway left off the lane and keep climbing until the road begins to level out. Here you will find the broad entrance to Portesham Farm on the left, about 500m from the start of Winters Lane with a bridleway signed along the well-surfaced drive to the farm. Take this and keep going up – the views to your right open up and are seriously good. You will also pass on your left an information board about the history of quarrying in the area and the view from this spot, guarded by a wonderful, gentle-faced stegosaurus made out of defunct farm machinery!

Continue uphill past the dinosaur and as the drive bends left and levels out you will see the farm buildings ahead, high up beyond them is the mighty structure of the Hardy Monument, where you will be later. At this point (grid ref: SY611859) you will also see a gate on the right with the remains of a yellow footpath arrow. Go through here and walk through the field with an old stone wall to the left. You are walking along a ridge with vast views to your right – Chesil Beach, with the water of The Fleet just inland of it, makes up part of the view. Follow this line until you reach a fenced enclosure with young trees planted within. This is the final resting place of a former owner of the farm who chose her spot well for its glorious views. What a lovely place to end up.

Below the enclosure the footpath leaves the field at a stile. Beyond the stile keep ahead with the ground dropping away to your right – you are heading just very slightly south of due west along this stretch. The substantial Waddon House will be visible amongst trees below to the right. Exterior shots of this were used in *Far from the Madding Crowd*. Keep on in the same line to another stile, cross here and continue as before. You eventually meet a stony crossing path with a stone wall in front of you. Go right, then left round the end of the wall and continue in the same direction as before, some very broken-down arrows (at the time of writing) confirm that you are in the right direction. The mound of Corton Hill is ahead of you.

At the end of the field you reach a double stile. Beyond here be careful and read the rest of this paragraph before starting the descent! The public footpath goes obliquely right, steeply down, and passing through the remnants of an old hedged boundary which straddles down the hill. This line reaches a stile at the bottom of the field beside the lane but this is a treacherous descent. From observation it appears that walkers tend to take a more winding route from the ridge down to the stile, although that's not what the footpath does. The stile, when you get

Bridleway approaching Portesham Farm

View from Portesham Farm   *St. Bartholomew's Chapel*

there, is quite high above the lane — cross with caution and turn left along the road.

You reach a T-junction with Coryates to the right and a footpath going straight ahead. Take this, it's part of the Jubilee Trail — presumably the Queen's Golden Jubilee, although, coincidentally, we were walking it during the weekend of the Diamond. Keep ahead with the rising ground of Corton Hill to your left, the path climbs slightly but not steeply as you skirt the hill and there are frequent arrows to guide you through this stretch. Soon you see the lovely hamlet of Corton with the delightful, Grade II* listed St. Bartholomew's Chapel which dates back to the 13thC, although there has been later rebuilding and restoration. The Jubilee Trail passes above the chapel but a gate gives access to its environs and it is usually open for visitors.

After your visit return to the Jubilee Trail and leave the field through the metal gate in the boundary, above and beyond the chapel. After this a narrow path leads to a concrete farm track. Turn left up it and at the lane turn left again away from the pylons, thankfully. (Try to ignore them and be glad of what happens when you press a light switch.) Follow the lane now for 650m, ignoring the first bridleway to the right which will take you under the wires not once but three times, and we don't think you want that! This is a nice, easy stretch of lane walking.

The lane starts to descend and enters trees. When you see a clearly signed footpath going right, take it. It climbs steadily, passing a bridleway on the left and continuing up the field with the boundary on the right. Continue ahead through a second field and as you enter a third field a yellow arrow directs you right. Follow this a short distance to a stile in the corner. Cross this, enter the field and turn left, following the boundary on the left hand side – at the time of writing the arrow on the stile was misleadingly pointing straight on, but you need to go left uphill here with pylons running roughly parallel, in the distance to your right.

Beyond the top of the field you'll notice some dominant grey hardware. Go left over the stile just before the top of the field then immediately right, crossing the mounds of a rather busy badger sett. You reach a fingerpost pointing back down to Coryates and here you go left along a broad track across Bronkham Hill. This is the South Dorset Ridgeway which has superb views from it. Look out for ancient tumuli to the right of the path.

At a gate ignore the footpath left to Hell Bottom and continue to a three-way fingerpost. Keep straight on here through another gate and towards the Hardy Monument, now just one mile away. Beyond the gate follow the line of the fence on the left, a blue bridleway arrow directs. At the next gate the Ridgeway path narrows and becomes fenced on both sides, continuing in the same direction to eventually be joined from the left by the Jubilee Trail (SY620873). Ignore any of these junctions and keep straight along the main path until you drop to reach a lane, 2km after joining the Ridgeway.

The Dorset County Council land of Blackdown is ahead of you. Go left on the lane and within about 30m go right on the footpath, still heading for the monument and crossing a plank bridge followed by a stile. Continue after a second stile, climbing to the lane. Cross the lane and immediately opposite the path forks. The right hand fork is what you need, leading to a fingerpost 20m away, so make a mental note of this but first visit the massive bulk of the monument, now in the care of the National Trust. Take a moment to peruse the heaps of information boards situated around the site. If you're lucky you'll also find a van here selling tea and coffee. The panorama is superb – Chesil Beach, the Isle of Portland, Bronkham Hill and the Ridgeway along which you walked earlier.

Leave the monument and return to the aforementioned path from the lane to the fingerpost. This states 'inland route', follow its direction, crossing the stony

Admiral Sir Thomas Hardy

Portesham is well-known for being the home of Admiral Sir Thomas Hardy who served under Nelson for several years. In 1803 he was appointed Captain to the flagship, HMS Victory. Hardy was at Nelson's side during the Battle of Trafalgar in 1805, where Nelson was fatally wounded and uttered those immortal words "Kiss me, Hardy". Born at Long Bredy in 1769, Hardy later resided at Portesham House. He died in 1839 and in 1844 this huge monument on Blackdown Hill was erected in his memory. It came into the care of the

National Trust in the 1930s. This Thomas Hardy is not to be confused with the well-known Wessex author of the same name whose novels are set in Dorset. From this elevated spot you can see most of Dorset, the English Channel and the Isle of Wight.

track and continuing on the trodden path beyond – a small stone waymarker reiterates 'inland route' and also tells you that you're heading towards West Bexington. The monument is over to your left now and you are heading in a south west direction towards the sea. At the next crossing path keep ahead, still on the inland route and going downhill away from the monument and towards woodland. This drops to a three-way fingerpost. Go left, downhill, to a post about 50m away with a blue bridleway arrow. Don't fork left here but keep ahead in the direction of the arrow, entering the woodland.

Keep going for almost 250m at which point, just after a left bend, look out for a fork in the path (grid ref: SY609870). Left goes uphill but you need to go right downhill here. Drop down for 150m to reach a broad crossing track with a three-way fingerpost on the left (a bit overgrown when we saw it). Go left here, approaching the ruined Blackdown Barn (grid ref: SY609868), another distinctive location in *Far from the Madding Crowd*.

Follow the track as it swings right between the ruins. Another fingerpost points you along a track towards Portesham. Follow this, heading uphill, and less than 150m from the barn look for the gate on the right, beside trees. A blue bridleway arrow is on the post to reassure you.

Go right off the track here and walk through the field with the copse to your left along a clear track. The trees peter out and you reach a gate into a second field, still continuing in the same line. Fabulous views here – behind to the monument, and ahead to Chesil Beach. Portesham is below you. The track bends left then right and continues to descend beside the right hand field boundary. Pass through a gate at the bottom and follow the track ahead to the road.

The final stage of the walk turns left along the road back towards the village. As the road swings left a brief diversion ahead along Back Street will bring you to the delightful village pond, awash with ducks and geese. Return to the main road, the embrace of the Kings Arms and your car.

Studland, Old Harry & the Agglestone

Distance: 6.8 miles / 11km

Studland is an Old English word meaning 'cultivated land where horses were kept' and nowadays a different kind of horse thrives here. The sheltered waters of Studland Bay are home to seahorses who live on the seagrass growing underwater. Although you won't see them on the walk it's lovely to know they are there. This is a spectacular route and relatively non-strenuous, having just a couple of uphill stretches that aren't too challenging. It goes past the most easterly end of the Jurassic Coast and offers the kind of scenery one would expect in this area. As with all coastal walking you need to be careful near the precipitous edges. The stretch along the Purbeck Way is airy and fabulous – but you do need clear conditions. The inland section also provides some rather striking rocky bits. This walk makes for a glorious day out and is brilliant for birds – with the possible treat of ring-necked parakeets, which we heard calling to one another in the tree canopy near the car park at the end of the walk.

Map: OS Explorer OL15 Purbeck & South Dorset 1:25 000

Start point: From the National Trust's Middle Beach Car Park in Studland. Post code: BH19 3AP. Grid ref: SZ035828

Directions to start: Studland is a village located on the Isle of Purbeck in Dorset. It is approximately 3½ miles to the north of Swanage and can be accessed from the A351 via the B3351

Parking: Middle Beach Car Park as per start point above

Public Transport: The only bus service passing through Studland is the number 50 operated by Wilts & Dorset. Timetables available online at www.travelinesw.com. Nearest railway stations are Poole (5½ miles) and Parkstone (5½ miles)

Distance: 6.8 miles

Refreshments: Joe's Café, Studland Beach, 07931 325243; Manor House Hotel, Manor Road, Studland, 01929 450288; Middle Beach Café at the southern end of the beach, 01929 450411

Toilets: At both Middle Beach and Studland Beach

Nearby places to stay: A Great Escape Guest House, 6 Argyle Road, Swanage, 01929 475853; Manor House Hotel, Manor Road, Studland, 01929 450288; The Old School House, School Lane, Studland, 01929 450691

Nearby places of interest: Brownsea Island (NT), Poole Harbour, 01202 707744; Corfe Castle (NT), The Square, Corfe Castle, 01929 481294; Durlston Castle and Country Park, Lighthouse Road, Swanage, 01929 424443; Swanage

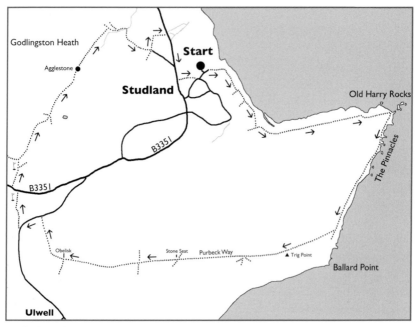

Railway, Station House, Swanage, 01929 425800
Possible birds include: Blackbird, buzzard, carrion crow, chaffinch, chiffchaff, collared dove, dunnock, goldfinch, great spotted woodpecker, green woodpecker, jackdaw, kestrel, magpie, nightjar (but only at dusk), oystercatcher, pied wagtail, gulls of various hue, ring-necked parakeets, shag, skylark, song thrush, stonechat, swallow, swift, tern, wheatear, willow warbler, woodpigeon, wren, yellowhammer
Authors' tip: Consider a visit to Brownsea Island. Dramatically situated in Poole Harbour it is a stronghold for the rare red squirrel
Note: Be aware: part of this route is across open moorland, so a map and compass are needed – and clear weather conditions

From the vehicular entrance to the car park cross the lane which goes down towards the beach and beyond it you'll see a path with a rounded stone waymarker directing you to the coast path, Fort Henry and Old Harry Rocks. Follow the path beneath trees and soon you reach the buildings of Fort Henry, an active place during WWII as the information boards here will explain.

Follow the path beyond and you reach an option where the coast path splits, either right inland or left on an alternative path along South Beach. Go left down the steps towards the beach, the descending path here can, in summer, be spectacular with plumes of foxgloves. On the beach (dogs on leads please) turn right and walk along the back of the beach, you see the white Old Harry Rocks on the headland in front of you. After about 200m along the beach look for the path ascending right and follow it as it continues under trees. It emerges from the trees at a three-way fingerpost (grid ref: SZ041823). Go left on the coast path towards Old Harry on a track which soon opens up into a field. Keep going for just under a mile – a lovely stretch of walking – following this line until you reach the headland of Handfast Point, with Old Harry Rocks just offshore. The gap between the headland and Old Harry is known as St. Lucas' Leap. This is the start of the Jurassic Coast.

Savour this astonishing area of rock stacks and pinnacles – but exercise caution on the edges please. Beyond Old Harry, follow the coastline with the sea to your left, remembering to glance back along the coast from time to time – the views are good there too. The area you are walking through is called Old Nick's Ground. Just over half a mile from Old Harry you will find a bridleway (with a not-very-clear blue arrow) forking right off the coast path through a gate. Go through here, walking diagonally right on the well-trodden path. This is the Purbeck Way and as you climb to reach a trig point 500m from the gate (grid ref: SZ044813), you will have superb views to your right over Studland Bay, Poole Bay and Poole Harbour where you will see Brownsea Island. Swanage Bay is to your left. The inland views are good too. Pause by the trig point to enjoy them.

Old Harry Rocks

Approaching the obelisk

You now follow the Purbeck Way westward across Ballard Down for almost 1½ miles, ignoring any turns off until you reach a rather elegant and unmissable stone obelisk. On the way there you will pass occasional gates, stone waymarkers, fingerposts, a small stone and wood bench and a much larger stone bench over to the right which earns a mention on the map! Pass all these features, keeping on the main west path until you reach the obelisk at grid ref: SZ022813. This rather modern-looking and attractive construction was built to commemorate the provision of a fresh water supply to Swanage in 1892. It was dismantled during WWII so as not to be a landmark for possible invaders and was later re-erected.

From here, ignore the turning left signed for Ulwell and follow the bridleway towards the B3351. Drop down to the road and turn left along it for 250m, walking along the verge on the right. As the road bends left you will see a public footpath sign just before a farm gate on the right. Take this, crossing the stile and climbing diagonally up the field beyond (north), walking away from the fence on the left and the hedge which conceals the road on the right. As you climb glance up to see the obelisk on the hill to your right.

You reach a stile and enter a copse. Emerge from the trees and you will find yourself on a golf course. A yellow-arrowed post directs you to another post a short distance away, and thence to a stile leading out onto the lane, there's another good view of the obelisk here. Turn left along the lane for less than 100m then turn right on the bridleway across the National Trust land of Godlingston Heath. Again you will be sharing the area with golfers. Keep on this track, ignoring any gates off, and in 150m you reach a bridleway forking right, which you don't want. (There is a sign here advising you to keep to the bridleways through this area of golf course.) Keep ahead on the main, clear track and about 100m after the fork, at grid ref: SZ018821, keep a sharp look out for a stone waymarker indicating that the bridleway goes left off the main path. Go left here. You are now heading for Agglestone.

You reach a substantial set of double gates with a stone waymarker about 25m beyond them. There is a meeting of ways here at grid ref: SZ020824. Keep going on the bridleway signed for Agglestone, which is ahead and slightly left. As you follow this clear track you will see Old Harry out to the right and the Isle of Wight further east. Suddenly you see the mighty, sandstone Agglestone Rock, quite a surprise when approached from this angle. Iron oxide deposits add to the colour. Legend suggests that the devil threw the Agglestone from the Isle of Wight in an attempt to hit Corfe Castle. In reality it is a naturally occurring stone that has toppled over.

The Agglestone on Godlingston Heath

Old Harry and the Jurassic Coast

The Jurassic Coast, England's first natural World Heritage Site, totals some 95 miles of Dorset and East Devon coastline stretching from the chalky white Old Harry Rocks in the east, which is the youngest (Cretaceous) section at 65 million years old, to Orcombe Point near Exmouth in the west, the oldest (Triassic) at 250 million years. The coast along this whole stretch, which tilts towards the east, is comprised of rock formations reflecting this 185 million year span of the Earth's geological history –  Cretaceous, Jurassic and Triassic. These rocks formed in a warmer clime than the Dorset of today and are not necessarily in chronological order as some 'young', Cretaceous rocks can be found amongst the old Triassic rocks in the west near Orcombe Point. Old Harry Rocks would have once been part of a system of caves which eroded to form arches and subsequently collapsed to form these stacks. Legends vie with one another to attribute the name to either the devil or a local smuggler, Harry Paye.

The Agglestone with human perspective!

Beyond the Agglestone a yellow arrow directs you down steps along a clear path back towards Studland. Wind your way for over 500m, crossing occasional plank bridges – it can be quite damp through this area. You reach a crossing, stony track at grid ref: SZ026831. Turn right, downhill towards trees, and you reach a bridleway at grid ref: SZ027831 – the post is low down to your left and easy to miss.

Turn right here, under trees and through an area of busy, babbling streams. You reach a footbridge on the right. Cross it and head over to the gate a short distance away, leaving Godlingston Heath and still following the clear bridleway beyond the gate. After about 150m you reach a cottage on the left. Continue on the track beyond here for just over 100m to a crossways with a plethora of blue bridleway arrows on a post.

Go left here, straight across the field for 125m to a post with a blue arrow. From this go right to reach a gate in another 125m. This leads onto the road. Turn right along the road, looking out for traffic, there are verges for safety. Follow the road for 400m and after Coombe House on the left take the footpath left. This shady way leads to the lane along which you turn left to arrive back at Middle Beach Car Park.

Worth Matravers, St. Aldhelm's & Dancing Ledge
Distance: 8 miles / 13km

Starting in a very attractive village, this is a reasonably easy to follow route of magnificent coastal scenery and some interesting and mighty quarry workings, an integral part of the history of the area. The romantic and beautifully-situated St. Aldhelm's Chapel is reached by a muscle-pinging climb of 218 steps – an excellent workout, be prepared to warm up! The delightfully-named Dancing Ledge is another wonderful place so make sure you save some picnic to enjoy there. The wildlife is good throughout and includes a habitat for great crested newts.

Map: OS Explorer OL15 Purbeck & South Dorset 1:25 000

Start point: From the car park in Worth Matravers 150m north of The Square and Compass pub. Post code: BH19 3LE. Grid ref: SY974776

Directions to start: Worth Matravers is a village situated approximately 3½ miles to the west of Swanage. It can be accessed from the B3069

Parking: For a small charge you can park all day in the village car park (see start point)

Public Transport: The only bus service passing through Worth Matravers is the number 44 operated by Wilts & Dorset. Timetables available online at www.travelinesw.com. Nearest railway station is Wareham (7.4 miles)

Distance: 8 miles

Refreshments: The Square and Compass, Worth Matravers, 01929 439229; Worth Matravers Tea and Supper Room, 01929 439368

Toilets: In the car park

Nearby places to stay: A Great Escape Guest House, 6 Argyle Road, Swanage, 01929 475853; Chiltern Lodge, 8 Newfoundland Close, Worth Matravers 01929 439337

Nearby places of interest: Corfe Castle (NT), The Square, Corfe Castle, 01929 481294; Durlston Castle and Country Park, Lighthouse Road, Swanage, 01929 424443; Swanage Railway, Station House, Swanage, 01929 425800

Possible birds include: Blackbird, carrion crow, chaffinch, chiffchaff, collared dove, dunnock, fulmar, goldfinch, gulls of various hue, house sparrow, jackdaw, kestrel, robin, skylark, stonechat, swallow, swift, whitethroat, woodpigeon, wren, yellowhammer

Authors' tip: A visit to the Square and Compass public house is a must. It's a little out of the ordinary as not only is it a very decent pub, it also houses a fossil museum on site. Additionally the pub hosts a two-week long annual stone carving festival from the end of July

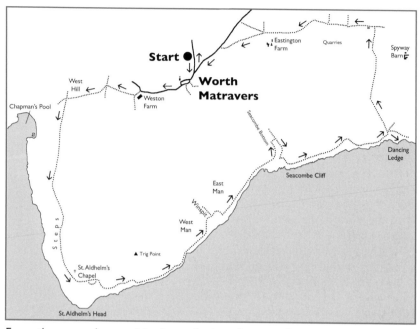

From the car park turn right down the lane. Ignore a footpath on the right and pass The Square and Compass pub (named for its quarrying connections) on the left. At the T-junction go right and walk through the village, passing the pretty area of the village pond with its Aylesbury ducks on the left. If you have time to pause and enjoy this area it's a good thing to do.

The walk goes uphill beyond the pond, bending left when it reaches the ancient Church of St. Nicholas on the right. Follow the road as it then bends right at the village hall and continue for 500m, ignoring footpaths to right and left until you reach Weston Farm. Here, beyond the barns, you will find a footpath left off the lane. This tells you that St. Aldhelm's Head is 1½ miles away. Take this, following a concrete farm track between farm buildings and a cottage. In less than 100m, just before the left bend in the track, you will see a yellow footpath arrow pointing right through a gate. Follow its direction along a stony track with a stone wall on the left. Within 50m the stone wall on the left ends and you enter a field – make sure you're in the field nearest the wall you have been following (there are other fields to the right) and keep straight ahead through the field with the fence on your right. At the end of the field exit via a gate and enter a car park. On the left you will find another footpath leaving the car park and heading diagonally across the field towards the coast. This leads to a field boundary beyond which the same line leads to a gate with a view beyond of the coastline and the Isle of Portland. Here you join the coast path. Turn left, heading towards St. Aldhelm's Head, 1 ¼ miles away.

Admire the well-maintained and at times artistic wall to your left here. You may notice the memorial bench displaying part of a large ammonite as its back. As you proceed you will have a lovely view down to the right into Chapman's Pool with beautiful views inland behind this cove. James hopes to one day have a cove named after him – not sure how we'd arrange that but Clancy Cove does have a certain ring.... Anyway, keep going along the coast to a delightful and rather surprising Royal Marines Memorial Garden.

Continue beyond here until you reach descending steps. At the bottom, ignore the path left and ascend the steps ahead. Sorry. We survived, so you should too. At the top there are benches (all occupied when we got there, Grrrrr) but stagger along the path and across to the little square chapel to enjoy its shade or shelter, depending on the conditions. Respect any nesting swallows! There is a row of wonderfully remote coastguard cottages nearby and a National Coastwatch Institution lookout.

When you've recovered return to the coast path and the graceful, stainless steel memorial to the radar research undertaken here. Notice the ruins of the radar

Steps to St. Aldhelm's

Climbers at Dancing Ledge

St. Aldhelm's Chapel

buildings below the memorial. Paths lead down if you wish to explore but the walk continues on the coast path towards Winspit, 1½ miles away. The path travels quite close to the edge at times so watch your step along here. Just before Winspit you encounter substantial disused quarries which possess a certain craggy grandeur. Keep going and descend with the path and steps to a broad crossing track in Winspit. Go right, still on the coast path, signed towards Seacombe, ¾ mile away.

Uphill steps out of Winspit lead to a gate onto the National Trust land of East Man – the name of the hill to the left. Another 500m brings you to another gate, keep going and soon you pass yet more quarry remains. Stay with the coast path, passing through another couple of gates and eventually steps lead down into Seacombe Bottom. Ignore any paths off and keep on the coast path which is still signed for Seacombe as that's the name of the cliffs beyond here. Dancing Ledge is beyond these, one mile away. Throughout this stretch of coastline you will have sight from time to time of the lighthouse, away to the east at Anvil Point.

Keep going, passing through three gates. At the third gate a sign tells you that this is the National Trust land of Spyway Farm. Continue through the field beyond here – you will see Dancing Ledge down to the right, stretching out into the sea. At the end of this field you will find a distinct plaque on the seaward end of a wall, denoting various footpaths. Before choosing one, cross the stile and go down to Dancing Ledge – it's worth a visit.

Come back up from Dancing Ledge and, with your back to the sea, take the footpath signed diagonally left uphill towards Langton. There is more than one grassy path heading in this direction, take the one nearest the wall but heading diagonally left away from it towards trees. When you reach the scrubby trees continue up on a now narrower path, it can be sticky underfoot. The path brings you to a kissing gate with a stone waymarker beyond, which it would be easy to trip over. A yellow arrow on this directs you right (north), to follow the line of the wall on your right, towards Langton.

You'll see disused quarries over to your right as you climb and the rooftop of Spyway Barn. Away to your left is a cottage called Sea Spray. The path levels out to afford good views ahead. The Isle of Wight is out to sea to your right. Also to your right you can see the airy heights of Ballard Down and the Purbeck Way, which you encounter on the Studland walk.

A track meets you obliquely from the left, keep going and soon you reach a broad crossing track. Go left here, this is the Priests Way, passing a little pond on the left, home of the great crested newt. Keep on the main track, which is a blue-arrowed bridleway, ignoring any turns off and passing quarries. After 700m

Dancing Ledge

St. Aldhelm's Head

Part of the Jurassic Coast (see feature on Studland walk) and also known as St. Alban's Head, this remote spot holds much history. The Norman Chapel, dedicated to St. Aldhelm, the first bishop of Sherborne, has a mysterious past. Its square shape and the fact that its corners are aligned with the points of the compass is not common in religious

buildings, giving rise to speculation that it may not have originally been a chapel. However, the vaulting and the presence of ancient graves outside would suggest that it has always been a place of worship. Its use has been irregular over the centuries and it was in a state of disrepair during the 18thC, when it was shown on a map as 'St. Abbon's Chapel'. Extensive repairs were carried out during the latter half of the 19thC. The cross on the roof probably replaces an original beacon fire basket, evidence for which was uncovered during repairs to the roof. The chapel reopened in July 1874 and was regularly used until the early 20thC. Nowadays informal services are held on summer Sunday evenings. The altar is of stone from St. Aldhelm's Quarry and was consecrated by the Archbishop of Canterbury, Rowan Williams, in 2005.

This area was also the hub of radar research during the early part of WWII. The Radar Memorial, designed by local sculptor Tony Viney, represents intertwined radar dishes which resemble a fire basket – a fire beacon being a means of defensive communication which was a forerunner to modern radar (which links in rather appealingly with the beacon basket on the chapel). Research carried out on this site shaped the future technology which developed systems still in use today. The ruins below the memorial are the foundations for a system of radar called 'Chain Home Low' which operated on VHF and was able to track low-flying aircraft which the early-warning system, known as 'Chain Home', was unable to catch.

the Priests Way bends left. Remain with it, passing through a gate as you approach Eastington Farm. Beyond the farm the track leads to another gate with a fingerpost.

On this post look for the yellow arrow pointing left through the field and follow its direction to where you can see a gate leading out of the field 250m away. You are following the line of the wall on your left here, but missing out its bendy bit.

Leave the field through a footpath gate and cross the next field in the same direction to another gate. Here, cross over the concrete drive and pass through the gate immediately opposite to keep going in the same line as before to reach the road.

Turn left along the road and follow it into Worth Matravers – away to the left you can see the coastline along which you've already walked. You reach The Square and Compass on your right. A diversion here is sometimes necessary but just beyond the Inn you find a right turn leading back to the car park from whence you started.

Worth Matravers

Walk 9
Burton Bradstock & Shipton Gorge
Distance: 9½ miles / 15.3km

A wonderful combination of coastal walking, attractive villages and high, inland viewpoints combine to make this another Dorset spectacular. The route also benefits from plenty of refreshment opportunity. Be prepared for ascents. A map and compass are very useful to confirm your direction.

Map: OS Explorer OL15 Purbeck and South Dorset 1:25 000	
Start point: From car park. Post code: DT6 4RL. Grid ref: SY502885	
Directions to start: Burton Bradstock is a village in south west Dorset, located approximately 3 miles to the south east of Bridport. The start point can be found 1¼ miles to the east of Burton Bradstock along the B3157	
Parking: In the car park as described above	
Public Transport: Bus operators that pass through Burton Bradstock are: First in Dorset & South Somerset and Damory Coaches. Timetables available online at www.travelinesw.com. Nearest railway station is Maiden Newton (8.8 miles)	
Distance: 9½ miles	
Refreshments: Hive Beach Café, Beach Road, 01308 897070; New Inn, Shipton Road, Shipton Gorge, 01308 897302; The Three Horseshoes, Mill Street, Burton Bradstock, 01308 897259	
Toilets: At Hive Beach Café during their opening hours. Also in Burton Bradstock on the B3157 Common Lane, opposite the fuel station	
Nearby places to stay: Chesil Beach Lodge, Coast Road, Burton Bradstock, 01308 897428; Norburton Hall, Shipton Lane, Burton Bradstock, 01308 897007	
Nearby places of interest: Abbotsbury Subtropical Gardens, Bullers Way, Abbotsbury, 01305 871387; Abbotsbury Swannery, New Barn Road, Abbotsbury, 01305 871858	
Possible birds include: Blackbird, buzzard, carrion crow, chaffinch, chiffchaff, fulmar, great tit, gulls of various hue, house sparrow, skylark, swallow, woodpigeon, wren	
Authors' tip: Nearby Chesil Beach is the largest shingle ridge in the world and deserves further exploration. This striking setting encloses a tidal lagoon which is home to a variety of wading birds	
Note: Be aware: part of this route is across high, open land, so a map and compass are useful – and clear weather conditions	

Leave the lower area of the car park through the kissing gate adjacent to a big gate and follow the left hand option of the paths beyond it towards the sea. This is a well-surfaced path, stay with it, ignoring the right hand fork after about 100m.

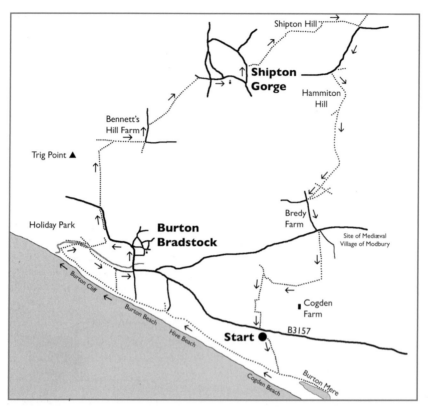

As you approach the sea you can glimpse Burton Mere over to the left. If you wish to visit the mere take the path going left towards it. The walk, however, continues to the right (west) along the coast path, away from the mere with the sea to your left. This is a delightful stretch of walking behind Cogden Beach. The grasslands beside the path are studded with wild flowers in spring and summer.

Continue beyond static caravans, ignoring any turnings inland, and keep on the coast path until you reach the café at Hive Beach. Here you could go straight past but we didn't, desiring to seek refuge from gale force rain on a glorious June day! Beyond here the walk continues along the coast, with views of Burton Bradstock over to the right. The cliffs climb and as you continue you will have striking views of the Jurassic Coast and beach ahead (see feature in Studland walk). Try to disregard the caravans.

Ignore any inland turnings until the path drops to a two-way fingerpost. Go right here signed for West Bay and Freshwater. You reach a three-way fingerpost and here you leave the coast path to continue straight on towards Burton Bradstock. There is an enticing depiction of a beer mug on the sign. This leads to a kissing gate on the edge of the village. Continue on the path beyond, there are some well-laid-out vegetable gardens over the wall on your left and you pass attractive cottages.

At the T-junction turn left and at the main junction keep left (which is effectively straight ahead) into the village along High Street. The road crosses the River Bride and bends its way through the village. Just beyond the end of the village, after the road bends right, look for the public footpath on the left enabling you to walk through the field beside the road, a rather safer option than walking along it.

At the end of the field cross the road with caution and pass through the farm gate opposite to continue on another footpath through this field, with the hedge to your right. This line brings you to a gate, keep going beyond it on the broad track, flanked by hedges. This emerges through another gate into an open field. From here follow the right hand boundary up to a stile within 100m. Cross the stile and glance back to enjoy the views and also to ascertain the line of the track you've just come along, as from the stile you need to walk straight up the field in this same line. You will notice the trig point over to your left, in the neighbouring field. As the rising ground levels out bear right across the field to a gate, exiting onto a broad bridleway. Turn right along it.

You reach the buildings of Bennett's Hill Farm at a meeting of ways. Go left here, passing the farm entrance on the left and following a track, Milvers Lane, for 200m at which point you will find a footpath going right. Take this, crossing the field as directed by the signpost towards Shipton Gorge. There are lovely views around you and the prominent, flat-topped Shipton Hill is ahead. This line leads to a double gate through the hedge, continue beyond it through four further fields, keeping the same line all the way – a lovely section of the walk.

Emerge from the final field onto a track. Turn right, heading towards the church tower. You swiftly reach a lane in the village of Shipton Gorge. Here the walk continues ahead along Port Lane (although you may first wish to go left for a few metres to make the acquaintance of the New Inn).

Follow Port Lane as it becomes Brook Street, looking out for gaps in the cottages on the right which afford good views of the church. You reach a phone box on the right and the entrance gate to The Orchard, once an overgrown apple orchard but now owned by the village and through which a path leads to the church if you wish to explore. Our walk continues past this, along Brook Street for another 20m, to a footpath going left.

Follow this path uphill to where stone steps take you up, away from a private garden and to a stile. Cross this and turn right, to follow the boundary on your right through the field. Before the end of the field a gap on the right leads you down to another stile and thence to the lane. Turn right along it, passing Small Coombe Farm, and a few metres further you reach a startlingly long fingerpost on the left. This one really doesn't want to be missed, so go left, as it tells you, towards Higher Sturthill. The track emerges into a field and you need to head diagonally left across the field to a stile in the opposite boundary. Pause to enjoy the view then cross the next field in the direction of the yellow arrow on the stile. This leads to another stile into a copse. Follow the path through the trees and at the next stile leave the trees to walk in the direction of the arrow, climbing through the field beside its left hand boundary as you approach Shipton Hill. This gets quite steep, keep going in the same line until you reach a gate in the top boundary with a yellow arrow.

Go through here and follow the arrow's direction, the fence is to your right with the hill rising to your left. Proceed until you reach a double stile. Beyond this continue in the same direction, climbing briefly, before magnificent views open up before you. Aim for the arrowed post ahead and continue beyond it, as directed by its arrow. (Before doing so you can, if you wish, explore the top of the hill along the path leading to its summit from this post.)

Walk away from the hill as directed to reach a stile to the left of a farm gate. Cross the stile then follow the hedge on the right for just over 200m until you reach a gate leading onto the lane. Turn right along the lane and keep going, admiring the views and noticing, to the left, the long and lofty hill fort of Chilcombe. Ignore any turns off until you reach the stone pillared entrance to Hammiton Farm on the left. Here a bridleway is signed along their drive. Take this and at the second set of grand gates you will see the bridleway veering right along a track, passing the farm buildings to your left. Hammiton Wood is beyond the farm with Hammiton Hill rising to the right.

The track reaches two gates, the right hand one bearing a blue bridleway arrow. Go through this and follow the left boundary of the field. At the end another arrow directs you straight across the field towards the right hand end of woodland, Eight Acre Copse. Reach the trees, keeping them to your left as you keep on in the same line to a gate. Beyond here follow the same line as before along the right hand boundary to another gate and then continue through the next field in almost the same direction – blue arrows on gates reassure you throughout this stretch so keep looking out for them.

At the next blue arrow follow its direction, heading diagonally right down the field in a south westerly direction. This brings you to a gate in a fence with trees to the right of the gate. Pass through and walk diagonally down the next field to its bottom right hand corner. Here emerge at a gate onto a track beside a lane.

Turn left along the lane, passing the beautiful house of Bredy Farm and crossing a small bridge over the River Bride. At the T-junction go left and in about 20m there is a footpath going right off the lane. Go through here – the fields to the left of the track are the site of the mediæval village of Modbury.

From the lane, ignore the track ahead and walk diagonally right across the field in the direction shown by the fingerpost. This is where a compass comes in handy. You are heading south at this point. This line leads to a stile in the corner – it was well-concealed and rickety at the time of writing. Cross here and walk up the next field with the hedge to your right. It then starts to go downhill and about 70m before the end of the field you will find a double stile on the right. Cross this.

Cliffs to the west of Burton Freshwater

From this point the footpath has been diverted and a year after the diversion some OS maps were still showing the old route. We are directing you on the new route, so it may not match your map.

Beyond the stile head down the field towards a pond, passing the corner of its fence on your right (your direction here is slightly south of west). Beyond the pond continue up the field in the same line, you will see the fence surrounding a disused pit up to your left. This line brings you to a gate in a stone wall on the far side of the field, enjoy the surrounding views as you go. A yellow arrow directs you west through the next field, bearing very slightly left to drop down to a gate

Lost villages

An apparently empty field is the site of what was once the village of Modbury and excavation has revealed pottery and the remains of buildings on both sides of the road. Mediæval buildings were frequently constructed of relatively non-durable materials such as cob which, if not protected from the elements, falls into decay and gradually disappears as far as the casual observer is concerned. Stone buildings, once abandoned, were often dismantled in order to re-use the stone elsewhere. Reasons for the desertion of villages vary from the pressures of trade and economy to the desire of a local, powerful landowner to relocate a settlement out of his view. There are about 20 lost villages in Dorset. Some remain as single farmsteads (see feature on Seatown walk).

The site of Modbury Village

in the corner of the opposite boundary. Beyond here keep going straight across the next field to its far boundary and another gate.

Here a yellow arrow directs you to bear right through the next field, going downhill. Follow this to a stream at the bottom where a solid stone track crosses the water, you don't have to wade. At the time of writing this was quite overgrown and the crossing point wasn't visible until you reached it.

Beyond the stream go right, following the bottom boundary of the field with the hedge to your right. In just over 60m this leads to a point with a gate over to the right at grid ref: SY502892. DON'T go right through the gate but instead turn left away from the gate, staying in the same field – you are on an overgrown, grassy track heading uphill (the council has indicated that better signage will be installed through here!). You will pass above the point at which you crossed the stream, now below to your left. Keep on up this track to the top right hand (south west) corner of the field where you will find a yellow arrow on a gateway. Pause a moment and look across the field ahead – a gate at the far side, diagonally left of where you are standing, is the point you need to reach, but the yellow arrow points you diagonally right as the footpath follows the right hand boundary all the way round the field to reach this gate. Get your bearings before you set off. (You're heading back towards the road from which you started so you may hear traffic and you can just make out the footpath fingerpost in the distance on the road.)

When you reach the gate on the far side of the field go through and walk up the next field, with the hedge on your left to reach the fingerpost in the corner. Go left and immediately right through gates to emerge onto the road (mind the traffic). Turn left on the road and your car park is about 50m along on the right.

From Shipton Hill

Walk 10
Charmouth, Seatown & Golden Cap
Distance: 6.8 miles / 11km

This superb, airy route starts with a beautiful inland stretch of walking past some idyllic farmsteads and returns along the Jurassic Coast (see feature on Studland walk), taking in the highest point on the south coast of England. The views are unrivalled, the paths well-maintained (mostly by the National Trust), the stiles dog-friendly and there are good refreshment stops. Don't let the ascents put you off – this is a real humdinger of a walk.

Map: OS Explorer 116 Lyme Regis and Bridport 1:25 000

Start point: Car park at the end of Stonebarrow Lane just east of Charmouth. Post code: DT6 6RA. Grid ref: SY381932

Directions to start: Charmouth is a village located in West Dorset approximately 3 miles to the east of Lyme Regis. It can be accessed via the A35

Parking: See start point (above)

Public Transport: Bus operators that pass through Charmouth are: First in Dorset & South Somerset and Damory Coaches. Timetables available online at www.travelinesw.com. Nearest railway station is Axminster (5.4 miles)

Distance: 6.8 miles

Refreshments: The Anchor Inn, Seatown, 01297 489215; Stonebarrow Shop and Information Centre (near the start)

Toilets: At Stonebarrow Shop and Information Centre (near the start)

Nearby places to stay: Bay Tree House B&B, Duck Street, Chideock, 01297 489336; Warren House, Main Street, Chideock, 01297 489996

Nearby places of interest: Bridport Museum, The Coach House, Gundry Lane, Bridport, 01308 458703; Dinosaurland Fossil Museum, Coombe Street, Lyme Regis, 01297 443541

Possible birds include: Blackbird, blue tit, buzzard, carrion crow, chaffinch, chickens (!), chiffchaff, goldfinch, great tit, green woodpecker, gulls of various hue, house sparrow, jackdaw, long tailed tit, magpie, pheasant, raven, robin, skylark, song thrush, sparrowhawk, stonechat, swallow, willow warbler, woodpigeon, wren, yellowhammer

Authors' tip: Charmouth beach is one of the best sites on the Jurassic Coast to go fossil hunting

Note: Be aware: part of this route is across open moorland, so a map and compass are useful – and clear weather conditions

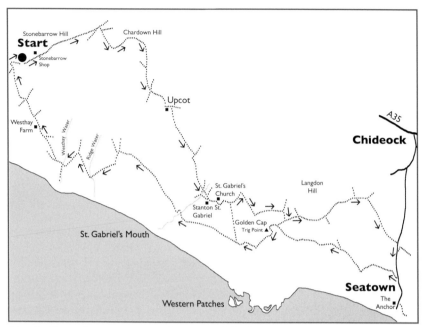

Not far from the entrance to the car park find the fingerpost pointing towards the bridleway at the far end of the car park from which the road entered. This directs you to the National Trust information and shop, Chardown Hill and Morcombelake. Follow this broad stony track beyond the car park enjoying the fabulous sea view to your right with the flat-topped hill of Golden Cap dominating the scene. Within 250m you reach stone-mounted information boards on the right of the track and the National Trust shop on the left, housed in a former radar station.

Beyond here continue along the track to where it broadens into another parking area, here you will find a four-way fingerpost. Take the bridleway pointing diagonally right towards the coast path going east, Chardown Hill and Golden Cap. This swiftly takes you to a gate beyond which you find a three-way fingerpost. Ignore the pointer to Chardown Hill and follow the direction indicated by the more right hand pointer, the option signed towards St. Gabriel's and Golden Cap. You are now heading for the sea in a south easterly direction. This is a wide grassy path which becomes a track heading downhill. Within about 200m of the fingerpost the track leads you through a lovely, treed boundary and a gateway with a stile beside it. Keep going, dropping downhill, with glorious views to the right. The track bends right and passes through another boundary, going through the right hand of two gates.

Keep going through yet another gate and soon you pass another fingerpost, keep ahead on the bridleway to St. Gabriel's. Spare a glance along the coast behind you as you progress – there is a good view back along the coast and towards the town of Lyme Regis. The path passes through the buildings of Upcot with its horses and hens – keep an eye on your canines.

Amongst the buildings look out for a two-way fingerpost at the corner of a wall on the left. Go left here towards St. Gabriel's and Morcombelake. Within about 100m look out for the footpath on the right and leave the track here, crossing the stile to walk straight ahead, passing a modern barn on the right, to another stile about 40m away. Cross this and follow the right hand boundary of the field you are now in, as indicated by the footpath sign. This brings you to another stile, cross here and turn right along the track beyond.

Within a few metres the track goes left, keep along it until you reach Stanton St. Gabriel. Here you will find a three-way fingerpost. Take the left option for Golden Cap and Seatown and soon you pass through a gate with an adjacent stile. The track leads past the well-preserved ruins of St. Gabriel's Church which you can enter for a look round. Beyond here follow the track to a three-way fingerpost about 50m away and then continue ahead in the direction shown towards Langdon Wood and Seatown (we go to Golden Cap later).

Through Upcot

View to Upcot from Golden Cap

Field path towards Seatown

The path rises and bends left, keep with it through this field, enjoying the views behind you when you pause for a breather. Golden Cap is up to your right now, at the end of the field pass through the boundary where there is a post with blue bridleway arrows. Turn right and walk uphill, following the right hand boundary as you approach the foothills of Golden Cap. Towards the top of the field you will see a stile on the right, ignore this and bear left, staying within the same field, to now follow its top boundary, keeping the boundary to your right with the sea behind you. In the top corner you find a three-way fingerpost with superb views beyond the gate. Your way lies ahead on the bridleway to Langdon Hill.

Walk across the field in the direction of the pointer enjoying the panorama towards Chesil Beach and the Isle of Portland. At the far side of the field pass through a gate to find another fingerpost. Keep straight ahead here towards Seatown and Chideock, with lovely coastal views to the right of the path and the wooded Langdon Hill up to your left. Beyond the woodland keep ahead on this tranquil path which is flanked by wild flowers in spring and summer. It has the rather curious name of Pettycrate Lane and you follow it for just over half a mile in total ignoring any stiles or turnings off it. The rooftops of Chideock come into view ahead – Seatown is the smaller cluster nearer to the coast.

Eventually the path passes lovely Seahill House on the left and then meets the road. Turn right.

Walk downhill along the road into Seatown. Before you get to the bottom of the hill you will see a path going right off the road, signed as the coast path diversion. This is the path you need once you've partaken of any refreshment you may require in Seatown. It is referred to as 'diversion' since the earlier path fell over the cliff – this is now the more stable option.

When you've finished in Seatown follow this coast path westward, you will see the white acorn waymarker. Pass through a kissing gate and continue on the clear path towards Golden Cap – so called because of the golden colour of the sandstone rock at its top which is strikingly beautiful when it catches the sun. Part of the Jurassic Coast, this mighty cliff is comprised of rock from the Jurassic and Cretaceous periods.

At the far side of the field go through another kissing gate, across a footbridge and through a small copse. Beyond here you will see a sign directing you towards the coast path, follow this. As you climb up out of Seatown remember to pause occasionally and look back the way you have come – the views along the coast are quite spectacular. When you reach a well-placed bench near a three-way

Golden Cap

Stanton St. Gabriel

A settlement has existed on this site since Saxon times and continued until the 18thC. At one time the main coach road ran near the village and many families lived and farmed hereabouts. The village became less frequented when a new road was built through Morcombelake and this was the beginning of the end for  Stanton St. Gabriel. Its residents moved away leaving their ghosts and memories behind. The nearby chapel is 13thC and was always difficult to maintain against the onslaught of the elements. It fell into disuse after another chapel was sited on the new main road in the mid 19thC – this more remote building subsequently becoming a handy store for smugglers' boodle. When this trade ended the chapel fell into disrepair. The surviving house dates back to the 16thC with later renovations and is now a National Trust holiday cottage. (See also feature on Burton Bradstock walk.)

fingerpost there's even more reason to pause. When you've had enough follow the finger that points you towards Golden Cap. Another kissing gate with a fingerpost gives you two onward options, take the left towards Charmouth – you're still approaching the unmissable Golden Cap with the sea to your left and Langdon Wood away to your right. Continue with this path until you reach the trig point at the summit – you are now at the highest point of England's south coast and a truly stunning view surrounds you. Crack open the apple juice.

From the trig point continue westwards, sea to your left, and soon you meet a stone-mounted memorial plaque to the Earl of Antrim, one-time chairman of the National Trust. The promontory of Golden Cap is to your left – enjoy its heights but be cautious on its precipitous edges.

Descend from the tops, still following the coast path heading west and dropping into a vista of patchwork fields with views over St. Gabriel's and, further away, Upcot, both of which you passed earlier. The town of Lyme Regis, with its Cobb jutting out into the sea, can be seen along the coast. Drop down to a three-way fingerpost from which you take the direction onwards towards Charmouth. As you progress along here you can see that the land to your left, above the sea, has slipped over the cliff. Don't follow it.

Continue on the coast path, descending trodden earth steps to reach more substantial wooden-edged steps which lead to a footbridge over a stream. Beyond here you have a stile with a four-way fingerpost. Keep straight on towards Charmouth, glancing back up towards Golden Cap from here and feeling grateful that it's behind you! The path leads to a gap in the hedge with a stile. Beyond this cross another field to another stile and continue, keeping strictly to the coast path through a succession of fields linked by stiles towards Charmouth.

As you progress look closely at the fingerposts as they frequently bear the grid reference and location on a small, white badge. Just over a mile from the point at which you started your descent from Golden Cap, you reach a three-way fingerpost bearing the name Ridge Barn/Broom Cliffs at grid ref: SY392926. Make the most of the adjacent bench – it has a good view of the final stretch of your walk.

From the Ridge Barn post head down the next field with a fence to your right and at the bottom of the field cross Ridge Water. Go up steps beyond it and at the top of the steps enter a field then bear diagonally right across it to another stile. Cross this and you find another fingerpost, this one denoting Westhay Water/Ridge Water on the badge. Ignore the right option to Stonebarrow Hill and keep on towards Charmouth. Descend another broad, grassy path to cross Westhay Water on the small footbridge. After this continue to a fingerpost, visible on the skyline.

When you reach this, the badge tells you this is Westhay Farm, grid ref: SY385927. Here you leave the coast path and bear right across the field for Stonebarrow Hill, as indicated. Walk towards Westhay Farm, and in the corner of the field, with the buildings to your left, you find a gate with a yellow footpath arrow. Follow the path, passing the house on your left – you're very close so respect their privacy. The footpath joins their drive, walk away from the farm along the drive, crossing a cattle grid and reaching a gate, beyond which the drive bends to the right. Here you will see a four-way fingerpost up to your left. Leave the drive and from the post follow the direction for the National Trust Stonebarrow Car Park.

This path takes you uphill for ¼ mile. Ignore any side paths, pass a stand of conifers on the right and about 100m beyond this a kissing gate leads you back into the environs of the car park from which you started.

Pilsdon Pen
Distance: 2¼ miles / 3.6km

Taking you to almost the highest point of Dorset (Lewesdon Hill is 2m higher), this short, spectacular walk is a must. It's easy to follow although be prepared for a couple of steep sections. Birdlife and history abound – Pilsdon Pen was an Iron Age hill fort situated in a strategic position of defence in the border territory of two Iron Age tribes, and the path across it is part of the Monarch's Way.

Map: OS Explorer 116 Lyme Regis & Bridport 1:25 000

Start point: From the parking area as described below. Post code: DT6 5NX. Grid ref: ST413009

Directions to start: Pilsdon Pen is a summit in West Dorset situated 4½ miles to the west of Beaminster. Leave the A3066 at Beaminster to follow the B1363 to Broadwindsor before continuing for a further 2 miles along the B3164

Parking: From the parking area below Pilsdon Pen on the B3164 at the junction of Pilsdon Lane. Post code: DT6 5NX. Grid ref: ST413009

Public Transport: Bus services in the area are operated by Dorset Community Transport. Timetables available online at www.travelinesw.com. Nearest railway station is Crewkerne (6.9 miles)

Distance: 2¼ miles

Refreshments: The Shave Cross Inn, Shave Cross, 01308 868358 ; White Lion Inn, The Square, Broadwindsor, 01308 867070

Toilets: None en route

Nearby places to stay: Crosskeys House, High Street, Broadwindsor, 01308 868063

Nearby places of interest: Broadwindsor Craft and Design Centre, Broadwindsor, 01308 868362; Forde Abbey and Gardens, Chard, 01460 220231

Possible birds include: Blackbird, buzzard, carrion crow, chiffchaff, goldfinch, gulls of various hue, house martin, jackdaw, magpie, pheasant, skylark, song thrush, swallow, swift, woodpigeon, wren

Authors' tip: Ensure you choose a clear day for this walk. Pilsdon Pen is a lofty summit and the views from its peak are breathtaking

Pilsdon Pen rises above the road and an obvious sign points you to the start of the walk on the opposite side of the lane to the parking area. Beyond the stile climb the well-trodden path to the top – this is all National Trust access land and part of The Monarch's Way. At the summit you will find a trig point and a wonderfully expansive flat area. There are views to everywhere.

From the trig point walk across the springy turf, crossing the full length of the fort until you reach the ramparts at the far end. Here bear slightly right to a

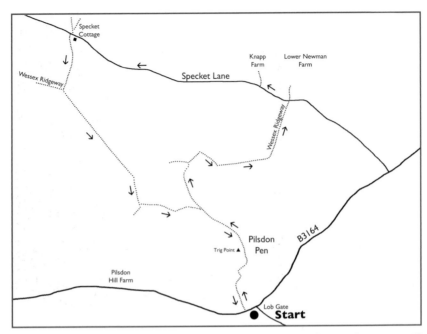

broad track exiting the fort. Beyond this head over to the fence where you will see arrows on a post. This is part of the Wessex Ridgeway, a 137 mile footpath following ancient trade routes – see feature on Plush walk. Turn right along it, keeping the fence on your left and heading downhill. You reach a gate leaving Pilsdon Pen, pass through and go right beyond it as indicated by the arrow. Keep going downhill on the path, the ground to your left slopes away and you have a bank boundary to your right. This path leads to a gate into a field, go left down the field to another gate which you can see in the bottom boundary. Here you will find the Monarch's Way emblem on the gatepost.

Pass through the gate and walk down the next small field with the fence on your left to emerge onto a lane. Turn left and follow the lane for almost half a mile, ignoring footpaths off until you reach Specket Cottage on the left. Just beyond it is a three-way fingerpost pointing you left to Pilsdon Pen again.

Go left here, up steps off the lane and through a gate. Beyond the gate follow the well-trodden path under trees to emerge up into a field. Bear left with the path, climbing up through the field with the boundary to your left. You reach a gate in the top left corner. Pass through, pause to admire the wonderful view behind then continue uphill in the same direction. You reach another three-way fingerpost by a gate and Pilsdon Pen is now ½ mile away.

Descending Pilsdon Pen

Trig on Pilsdon Pen at 277m above sea level

The Monarch's Way

The Monarch's Way is a 615 mile footpath following the escape route taken by Charles II in September 1651, after the Battle of Worcester. This is the route along which he fled from Worcester to Shoreham in Sussex, before sailing to France. The tree depicted on the Monarch's Way emblem is the 'Royal Oak' in Shropshire in which he hid to escape Cromwell's troops. The ship is The Surprise, a coal boat that carried Charles from Shoreham to France.

The creator of this long-distance path, Trevor Antill, died in 2010 and as a tribute his friends, the Minders of the Monarch's Way Association, carried his boots in relay the whole length of the route for one long, last walk.

Go through the gate and walk across the next field obliquely right in the direction indicated by the finger. This line takes you to a gate in the bottom boundary of the field. Beyond the gate go left on the track down to the corner of the field. Here another gate brings you to a meeting of ways. Go left and negotiate a rather flamboyant stile beside a gate bearing various carvings. You are now once more entering the area of Pilsdon Pen. Follow the path diagonally up, away from the stile and the boundary of rather striking trees adjacent to it. You are now climbing through the ramparts of the hill fort to once more reach the summit.

At the top turn right towards the trig point. From it, find the path to its left that you ascended at the beginning of the walk and retrace your steps downhill back to your starting point – watching for traffic as you once more cross the stile onto the lane.

Cerne Abbas & Buckland Newton
Distance: 7½ miles / 12km

Cerne Abbas is well-known for its chalk giant and although the walk goes right past him you can't see much from the path (see Author's tip). Allow time to explore Cerne Abbas, it is steeped in history and has plenty of interest. The village originally grew up around a 10thC abbey, the house is now privately owned. This is a reasonably easy-to-follow walk of high views and attractive villages.

Map: OS Explorer 117 Cerne Abbas & Bere Regis 1:25 000

Start point: Outside The New Inn. Post code: DT2 4JF. Grid ref: ST664011

Directions to start: Cerne Abbas is a village in central Dorset situated 8 miles north of Dorchester. It can be accessed from the A352 which runs close to the village

Parking: On street parking is usually possible in the village. Otherwise there is the Kettle Bridge Car Park off Duck Street at grid ref: ST663014

Public Transport: Bus number 216 operated by Damory Coaches. Timetables available online at www.travelinesw.com. Nearest railway stations- are Maiden Newton (4.6 miles) and Dorchester West (6.9 miles)

Distance: 7½ miles

Refreshments: Gaggle of Geese Buckland Newton, 01300 345249; New Inn, 14 Long Street, 01300 341274; Royal Oak, 23 Long Street, 01300 341797

Toilets: On Long Street in Cerne Abbas (opposite The Royal Oak)

Nearby places to stay: Abbots B&B, 7 Long Street, 01300 341 349; The New Inn, 14 Long Street, 01300 341274

Nearby places of interest: Cerne Abbey, Abbey Street, (no telephone); Cerne Giant (NT), 01297 489481; Tutankhamun Exhibition, High West Street, Dorchester, 01305 269571

Possible birds include: Chaffinch, chiffchaff, collared dove, house martin, house sparrow, pheasant, pied wagtail, robin, skylark, song thrush, swallow, swift, woodpigeon, wren, yellowhammer

Authors' tip: For those who wish to gawp at the Cerne Giant we recommend the viewpoint at the top of Duck Street close to the A352

From the main road (Long Street), turn up Abbey Street beside The Royal Oak. Pass the lovely Tudor houses of the Pitchmarket on the left and the church on your right with stocks outside. The entrance to the Squibb Garden is next to the church and this is good to visit if open. Continue to the end of Abbey Street, dominated by the beautiful Abbey Farm House. To the right of this is the entrance to Cerne Abbey. At 90° to the abbey entrance a stone-arched gateway leads into a graveyard and inside this gate a fingerpost gives you two options. Before taking

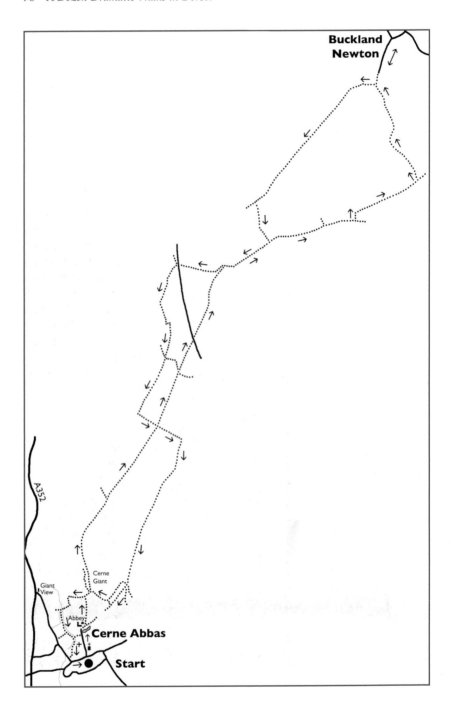

either notice the board on the wall to the right relating the legend of St. Augustine's Well.

Take the left path from here, heading for Giant's Hill (this is incised in the wooden post). The path soon exits the graveyard through another wrought iron gate. You are now in an open, grassy area, keep ahead, slightly uphill towards the trees, walking away from the wall surrounding the graveyard. This path rises to a stile under the trees. Beyond here seek out the four-way fingerpost at a meeting of paths (you will revisit this place later). Your way lies up the flight of steps in the direction of Giant's Hill.

At the top of the steps walk ahead, entering National Trust land. You pass the Giant's fenced enclosure on the right – if you peer up you can just about glimpse his feet! Although this area is access land you can walk round the fence you can't clamber about the Giant as he needs protection. Follow the path (the Giant Walk) beyond the enclosure enjoying views ahead and left. Ignore any paths off and keep going for 800m until you reach a stile. Cross this and go obliquely left through the field as indicated by the yellow arrow. In just over 250m you reach a four-way fingerpost beside woodland. Keep ahead on the footpath. (You'll be back here later on the crossing bridleway.) An expansive field is to your right with the boundary to your left. Within 300m you cross the Wessex Ridgeway (see feature

The Pitchmarket

on Plush walk), a fingerpost here states that Buckland Newton is three miles away. Keep on through the field and at the left corner cross the stile onto the road.

Cross the road diagonally left to another stile beneath trees. Head diagonally left across the field towards the far boundary, and when you meet the boundary turn left, keeping it to your right, and following it to the furthest corner of the field from where you entered off the lane. Here, just along on the left, you will find an exit onto a track, Barnes's Lane. Turn right along it.

Pass through a gate and keep on Barnes's Lane, passing a track on the left in 350m and another in a further 400m. Look out for these tracks on the left because just over 200m after the second one you need to watch out for a gate on the left. There are blue bridleway arrows by this gate but at the time of writing we had to peel the ivy off them and this will re-grow, so you may not see them. Go through the gate to enter the field. At this point there is a lovely view of the pale stone church in Buckland Newton, nestling in the valley in front of you.

Walk diagonally right (north east) down the field to the far boundary where you find a farm gate with a blue bridleway arrow leading onto a clear, stony path hedged on both sides. Follow this for 200m until you find a bridleway through a gate on the left. At the time of writing this bridleway was closed to horses and an active badger sett was signed nearby, but assuming you're not on horseback this is the path you need. So, go left through the gate and follow the line of the boundary on the right to reach a gate in the corner near barns. Beyond the gate follow the track past the barns and keep on the track as it bends right away from them. You reach a single-storey, red brick building in the environs of Knap Farm. Just before this notice the bridleway going left, as this is the route you need for your return to Cerne Abbas. For now, keep ahead to reach the lane at the entrance to Knap Farm, then follow the lane ahead into Buckland Newton.

The lane reaches a T-junction. Go right if you wish to visit the welcoming Gaggle of Geese, or go left if you wish to visit the church. Once you've finished in Buckland Newton retrace your steps along the lane to Knap Farm. Pass through its entrance and take the bridleway going right after the red brick building. This track quickly becomes mucky after rain but we did get through without going over our walking boots. The path climbs beyond the trees, pause from time to time to enjoy the views behind and as you climb higher the views around open up too. Keep going for over 1km until you reach a left turning with an adjacent barn. Go left on this track and within 300m you reach a T-junction beyond a gate. Go right– this is Barnes's Lane again. Retrace your steps for 350m to pass on the left the footpath that you came along earlier. Ignore it and keep going to reach the road.

Cross the road and opposite you find two bridleways signed on a fingerpost. Take the one ahead to Cerne Abbas, 1¾ miles away, walking in the direction shown by the post, with trees to your left, to another fingerpost about 50m away. This second post tells you that you're heading towards the Wessex Ridgeway on the Cerne Valley Trail. The path goes under trees, with the ground dropping steeply to your right – a lovely stretch of walking.

Keep on the path, you will find yourself following a fence on the left with trees to the right. You reach a metal farm gate, go left beyond it to climb up to a two-way fingerpost 20m away. From here turn right, still aiming for the Wessex Ridgeway and with the fence to your left. This brings you to a four-way fingerpost where the Wessex Ridgeway crosses. Keep straight ahead towards Cerne Abbas 1¼ miles away, the fence is still to your left with occasional glimpses of views through the trees to your right. 400m from the Ridgeway crossing the path leads to a small metal gate ahead (not the farm gate on the left). Go through the small gate and turn left after it on a narrow path. This rises beneath trees to a gate by a two-way fingerpost in 40m. Keep straight on beyond the gate, with trees to your left and an open field to your right. You reach a four-way fingerpost that you should recognise from earlier in the walk.

Go straight ahead on the bridleway, across the middle of the field to a gate at the far side. Beyond the gate go immediately right through another, still on a

Enticing path

Cerne Giant

The most unmissable feature on this walk is the 180ft tall, naked and over-endowed giant carved into the hillside. His origins are lost in the mists of time and vary from Saxon to 17thC, the latter being the most likely. He was made by cutting trenches through the grass and soil to reveal the chalk beneath. During the 1990s exploration indicated that the Giant had altered since his birth, at one time he carried a cloak over one arm and had a disembodied head at his feet. The site of the Giant is owned by the National Trust and he is re-chalked every couple of decades. Much folklore surrounds his origins, mostly connected with fertility.

Some years ago pupils at a girls' public school recreated the giant with a white-line machine, paying particular attention to one of his features. The reproduction was completed overnight, just in time for parents' open day.

bridleway and with the fence to your right, following a track. This reaches a two-way fingerpost. At it, go through the gate and follow the direction indicated by the finger, heading left and downhill. The land beyond the boundary on the left drops away with good views beyond. You may see roe deer in this area.

Descend with this track for 750m after which keep a sharp eye open for a fingerpost on the right, under trees, signed for 'abbey and village'. This takes you over a stile into a large field. Two yellow arrows are on this stile, you need the one pointing ahead, keeping the trees to your right. At the next fence cross the stile beside the trees and go right, as directed by the arrow. You are now under trees and quickly reach another stile. Cross here and turn left on the path beyond, the fence to your left. This reaches a meeting of ways where you find a familiar four-way fingerpost. Here keep ahead on the path towards Kettle Bridge, passing through a kissing gate and following a stony, downhill path beneath trees.

You reach a barn in just over 100m. Turn left to reach a T-junction in about 50m, with a barn conversion to the left. Go right, away from it, cross the river on a bridge and turn left after the bridge towards the village. Follow this, with the River Cerne to your left and keep ahead, ignoring a wooden footbridge to the left. Pass a gushing waterfall and the path arrives at Mill Cottage on the right with The Mill House on the left. Keep going to reach the junction of Mill Lane and Duck Street. Turn left along Duck Street to reach Long Street. Go left here to arrive back at your start point.